The Skier's Year-Round Exercise Guide

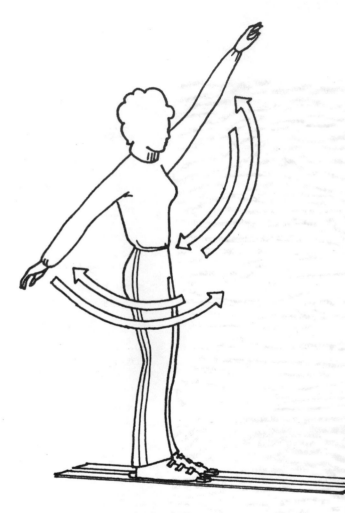

The Skier's Year

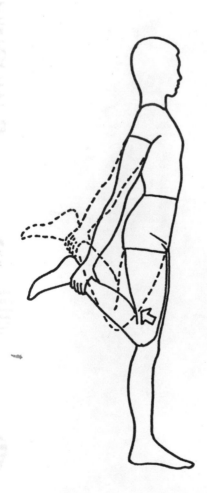

Round Exercise Guide

Safe, Effective Techniques for Men and Women

THEA DEE SLUSKY, R.P.T.

Illustrations by Joe White

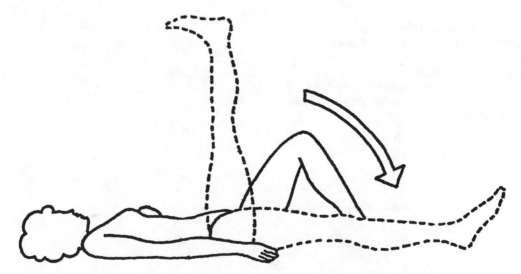

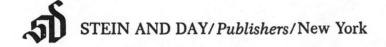 STEIN AND DAY/*Publishers*/New York

First published in 1979
Copyright © 1979 by Thea D. Slusky
All rights reserved
Designed by Ed Kaplin
Printed in the United States of America
Stein and Day/*Publishers*/Scarborough House,
Briarcliff Manor, N.Y. 10510

Library of Congress Cataloging in Publication Data

Slusky, Thea Dee
    The skier's year-round exercise guide.

    Includes index.
    1. Skis and skiing.   2. Exercise.   I. Title.
GV854.85.S58   796.9'3   78-7254
ISBN 0-8128-2512-8
ISBN 0-8128-6003-9 pbk.

This book is dedicated to my parents and my brother, Ronald.

ACKNOWLEDGMENTS

To Dr. Lila Swell, whose optimism, guidance and encouragement made this book possible.

Many, many thanks to the following people for their enthusiasm, and valuable suggestions:

Robert Greene, good friend and fellow skier

Hans Kraus, M.D., Medical Advisor, President's Council on Physical Fitness and Sports

Keichi Murata, Shiatsu Therapist and teacher

Willibald Nagler, M.D., Chairman, Department of Rehabilitation Medicine, The New York Hospital-Cornell Medical Center

Doug Pfeiffer, former editor-in-chief, *Skiing Magazine;* current contributing editor, *Ski Magazine*

Jacqueline Schuyler, R.P.T., physical therapist, The New York Hospital-Cornell Medical Center

Joe White, talented and patient artist

Contents

Introduction

The Skier's Year-Round Exercise Guide is a book for all skiers. It is also a book about human movement, both on and off the slope. This book is unique in that it will help you become more aware of the kinds of body motions used in skiing and then help you to apply this in your pre-ski conditioning.

It is important to recognize that many of the motions used in skiing are the same ones we rely on subconsciously every day. Even walking or getting up from a chair involves complex movement patterns which require a precision of balance, timing, and rhythm of all the body's parts. Skiing is balancing in motion. It relies on these very same skills of precise, coordinated motion.

In addition, skiing has strength, flexibility, and endurance requirements. Some of these are quite different from those things we do in our daily activities or in other sports. Knowing this will help you to see why skiing may feel awkward to the beginner and why without proper physical conditioning even the experienced weekend skier may wake up Monday morning with aches and pains.

First and foremost, skiing is an active sport. No amount of reading, talking, or thinking about it will prepare you adequately for its physical demands. Skiing is more than just sliding down a hill, and it involves a lot more than just the use of your legs.

Whether you are a downhill or a cross-country skier, this book will help you to plan a complete exercise program for yourself or to learn how to do exercises properly to supplement your own exercise routine. In fact, your non-skiing friends and relatives can also plan a program of exercise for their own general physical conditioning. You will learn how to test your physical fitness and design a program of exercises specifically suited to your needs. With the Basic Program you start at a level of exercise consistent with your physical condition and progress at your own rate. *This book will teach you* WHAT *exercises to do,* WHY *you are doing them,* HOW *to do them, and how* NOT *to do them.* It will help you to see that all exercises are not alike.

As you exercise in preparation for skiing you are becoming more and more aware of your muscles: how they feel, what motions are easy and natural for you, and how diverse your body positions can be. All of the sensations of muscular stretching, tightening, and relaxing that you experience in the Basic Program will be familiar to you when you're exercising and when you're skiing. Through exercising you're learning about your body and about yourself.

Think of this book as a study guide to teach you about yourself. Many people follow a regular schedule of dental and medical check-ups, but how many people give themselves a check-up for the general condition of their muscles and joints? When you take the physical fitness quiz in this book you won't need anyone else to point out your weak areas for you.

Everyone knows that exercise is important in helping people to live longer, healthier lives. It's rare to pick up any popular magazine today and not find advice on how to shape-up, stay-fit, look younger, and feel and look better. But, how many people do not exercise because they don't know what to do; and how many people do exercise but don't know what they're doing?

Today millions of Americans are getting involved in sports or other physical fitness activities at ever increasing rates. People are joining health clubs, jogging, cycling, playing tennis or squash, taking yoga and dance lessons. For some people the goal is to be physically fit by running further without getting winded, for others it's playing two hours of tennis without developing a backache, or completing 25 sit-ups.

This is all well and good. But, if you're a skier, you need special preparation. Special preparation means doing exercises that improve your strength and flexibility and endurance. You need them all, whether you're a downhill skier or a cross-country skier.

This is a serious book for people who are ready to be honest with themselves about their lack of physical fitness. It may change your ideas about the meaning of "fitness." It's a book for those who have the desire to improve and for those who are committed to putting forth the effort that is absolutely essential for good results.

To benefit from this exercise guide you don't have to be an experienced skier; in fact, you need not have ever skiied before. Simply, this is a book for all of you who care about yourselves and want to ski. It's a book to read and use as a guidebook. It's a book to refer back to again and again to keep your exercise program up-to-date as you make improvements or as your physical condition changes. Reading a book to learn about yourself and what to do for yourself is no different than reading a book to become a better chess or backgammon player. You can study the movements of your body the same way that you study the movements and strategies of the pieces on a gameboard. If you want to become more skilled at these games you can do so by learning more about their subtleties. If you want to become more skilled at exercising properly to achieve the best results, it helps to study about that, too.

The Skier's Year-Round Exercise Guide was written to enable you to experience and learn about yourself. It's designed to help you to be stronger and more flexible, get more out of your ski lessons, and have a more enjoyable day on the ski slopes.

T.D.S.

The Skier's Year-Round Exercise Guide

1 | | The Physical Demands of Skiing

Skiing is very special. It's fun, challenging, full of surprises and risks. It's for people of many different ages and athletic abilities. Skiing is for those who are aggressive as well as those who are more cautious. You can go fast on skis or slowly, take many turns to get down the slope or very few. There's the individual expression of style and pace that allows every skier to express himself.

For some, skiing provides the thrill and challenge to perform on an ever-changing surface; to test their reflexes and skill against the obstacles of the mountain. For everyone there's the opportunity for lots of pleasure. But, there's work involved in order to reap the pleasure.

It's hard to imagine skiing as work because we do it for recreation and enjoyment to give ourselves a sense of well-being and accomplishment and fun that comes with physical effort. But the work is there disguised as wedge turns and stem turns, parallel turns, jet turns, traverses, side steps, falling down, and getting up.

To get your skis to move where you want them to go, when and how you want them to go takes commitment. You must have the physical ability to get the skis to do what you think they should do. It's your condition which determines the quality of your skiing, whether you can partake in all of the bending, crouching, jumping, schussing, and sliding that it takes to ski for maximum fulfillment and pleasure.

Getting started on skis is a lot easier than it used to be. Short skis and rigid boots have taken care of that. Ski techniques are also easier because skiing is not as disciplined and stylized as it used to be. Today, greater emphasis is placed on doing things on skis that feel natural and comfortable.

Skiers today spend a lot of money on their equipment. They read all about the latest and newest in skis, boots, release bindings. They dress more beautifully and functionally than ever before. They are learning to maintain and fine tune their own skis in addition to having them done at a ski shop. They are taking ski lessons to get professional advice at all levels of ability.

What they all seem to have forgotten is to tune themselves up, to keep their own body machine in good working order, and to provide it with the proper running conditions and maintenance—just as should be done for any piece of complicated machinery.

No one should ski season after season without periodic checks of his safety bindings, bottoms, and steel edges. Then why go out without checking your own safety system? Your safety systems are the strength, flexibility, and endurance of your body to perform the maneuvers of skiing without unnecessary fatigue and strain. You can't expect your body to stay at a suitable level of performance if you don't activate it to stay that way.

Skiing is all about balance while in motion.

Everyone knows something about that, for it's part of the everyday moving and living that we're very used to. Balance on skis shares some common ground with these everyday activities, but it also has some significant differences that make specific physical conditioning for skiing especially important.

We know how to get up from a chair, how to walk down a flight of stairs, reach for something overhead or walk up a ramp. We do these things automatically without having to think about them. We've been moving around and walking and balancing in various ways since infancy, and we're adept at adjusting our center of gravity to keep upright and maintain our equilibrium.

Walking is a balancing activity consisting of a progression of taking a step, losing our balance momentarily and then regaining it as the following step reaches the ground. Many automatic reflexes and sensory organs in the body help us maintain equilibrium. There are sensory receptors in the ears, eyes, skin, muscles, tendons, and joints that give constant feedback to the brain. Messages from these receptors transmit sensations of pressure, pain, heat, and cold via the nervous system. In this way the muscular system can provide the appropriate action for the needs of the situation. You have receptors that tell you whether your elbow is bent or straight even if you close your eyes and can't see it. All of these mechanisms work for you while skiing. Only when your body is alert for sudden changes can you react to all the changing stimuli around you. Your body is influenced by many different things when skiing, such as the type and condition of the snow, the pitch of the slope, the irregular contours of the terrain, the temperature, wind, and sun. The less tense you can keep your muscles, the more able you'll be to respond the way you need to, and the more enjoyable your skiing will be.

To ski enjoyably the development of a sensitivity and awareness of your body is necessary. The better you feel changes in weight, the position of your center of gravity and varying pressures on your muscles, the easier it is to improve your technique. You should be able to sense in your body what it feels like to have more weight on the ball of each foot or on the heel, or to feel the tension in the muscles of one hip when you are putting weight only on that leg. Exercising helps develop awareness for some of these feelings of muscles being tensed or relaxed, stretched or strained. When you walk, there is a flow of motion in your legs that you don't have in downhill skiing. Skiing too has a grace and flow of motion, but as you will see, a very different type of muscular work is used. When walking, the legs swing freely like pendulums to take advantage of the natural push-off from each step to the next. Normal walking places little stress on the arms, which dangle freely or swing to and fro with the cadence of the steps.

That slight swing of the arms is an important feature of smooth walking. Try to walk with one hand resting on your back or on top of your head, and you'll immediately sense that your balance is off a little. Try to ski with the arms tense and resisting the flow of movements, and your balance will be altered also. Anything you do that strains your balance calls up extra muscular work, and that means unnecessary fatigue.

Of course a skier doesn't swing arms and legs to and fro as in walking. Skiing movements are more limited. They are maintained in a particular relative position to insure stability. Some skiing movements are more exaggerated than in walking, however, because the length of the skis gives leverage to the body that it doesn't have otherwise. For example, with skis on you can lean further backward and forward without falling over by using your upper and lower leg muscles in new ways. So it is that many of the balancing, moving, and holding motion patterns of the skier place vigorous and unfamiliar stresses on the muscular system. And so a physical conditioning program for skiing needs to take this into consideration. The kinds of twisting, turning, and stretching movements of skiing and the falls that come with skiing should be part of the physical conditioning program.

Obviously, skiers need strength and flexibility in ways different from normal daily requirements. Many of these movements and rotations aren't unique to skiing. In fact, the same principles and exercises apply for baseball players, tennis players, discus throwers, and skiers to generate torque for power and speed. However, each sport also has its combination of specific demands that make it unlike any other sport. That is why a well-trained swimmer does not necessarily have the adequate physical conditioning needed for skiing. In addition, getting into better physical condition by doing only one particular type of exercise such as jogging does not provide adequate conditioning for the type of muscular strength and flexibility needed on skis.

Skiing, like almost all human movement, involves combinations of stability and mobility of the body parts; thus, while some muscles are working to support one part of the body, they also provide another part with the freedom to move functionally. In eating, for example, the shoulder and elbow provide support to position the arm in space while the forearm, hand, and fingers move to and from the mouth. When you take a step, the muscles of one hip keep the pelvis level so that the other leg is free to clear the ground.

Similarly, your muscular system has diversified jobs to do while you're skiing. However, one of the things that is particularly strenuous about skiing is that the muscles must either hold a part of the body in the same position for a long period of time or else work continuously without the type of rest phase that usually accompanies rhythmical work. If you swing an axe or a golf club, ride a bicycle, or run up a hill, there is a definite alternation in the direction of your movements that allows different sets of muscles to work and relax. When you ski, you are always depending on the bending action of your legs to support and move you. You are usually positioned with your feet directly underneath your body or out toward the sides. Your trunk is relatively quiet, while your hips provide the leg movements to turn your skis. This is why skiers experience so much soreness in the muscles of their thighs and hips when they haven't had adequate physical preparation for these unusual stresses in skiing. In addition to strength for sustained muscular work, the same muscles must be able to elongate for the awkward positions a skier may find himself in when he falls. That is why the exercise program presented in this book teaches you both strengthening and stretching positions.

The basic demand on the muscular system is similar for all skiers, regardless of ability or skill level. Everyone on skis is subjected to the force of gravity, as well as the centrifugal force that tends to throw the skier's balance to the outside of a turn and the fluctuations and inconsistencies in the surface of the ski slope. Modern ski equipment has made it much easier for skiers to turn, apply pressure to, and edge their skis. The higher, more rigid plastic boots make it easier for small movements and small forces from the legs to be transmitted immediately to the skis. Still, it is the *skier* who must apply his body weight along the length of the ski, position the ski on its flat bottom or steel edges and apply leverage in the right amount at the appropriate time.

A skier has to have a reasonable degree of

physical conditioning. No, you don't have to be a super-athlete, but you do need a combination of strength, flexibility, and endurance to execute the maneuvers that are part of modern ski technique,

Why strength? Well, for a start let's say that you're a beginner. Part of your expectations for your first few attempts on the slope should include falling. There's nothing unusual about falling. In fact, it's common at all levels of ability. However, it takes strength to keep getting up again.

Strength is also required to maintain control over your skis. Getting them to glide along the snow is easy; that's what they were designed to do. Stopping, though, particlarly for beginners, is hard work requiring muscular effort. The natural tendency of a ski is to follow the fall line and shoot straight downhill. To turn it across the hill to increase friction between it and the snow takes muscular effort too. The steel edges, side cut, and camber of the ski all make it possible for the ski to perform well on the snow as long as the skier provides the energy. With a firm muscular system, a skier can weight and unweight his skis, shift his weight from one ski to the other and direct it toward the tip, center, or tail of the ski. These necessary pressure changes require firm muscular effort and control.

Subtlety of control over skis comes with experience. Inexperienced skiers use excessive body motion to throw their hips and shoulders into each turn, thinking that the more total effort they put out, the more proficient their skiing will be. Such skiers become easily fatigued and easily discouraged. The skilled skier is the one who has developed the efficiency of his muscular efforts to use only as much effort as is required to minimize fatigue and improve performance.

If muscular control is lacking, a skier may hesitate to lean full body weight onto both skis or carry it all on one leg and steer the ski with leg rotation. There are times when one ski may be sliding and the other one biting the snow. The hesitant skier may lean back toward the hill for security or simply lack the strength to sustain an edged ski all the way across a hill.

Advanced skiers also require strength, but for reasons far different from those required by beginners. Skiing at high speed in the bumps, making short stops, and stepping and skating with rapid changes in direction place lots of stress on skiers' muscles. In fact, advanced techniques are not really complicated, but many intermediate skiers simply are not physically capable of performing them.

Skiers need strength and flexibility so that the muscles have the ability to elongate adequately. Flexibility also improves the ability of muscles to contract. Muscles that stretch easily permit the body to move quickly and without strain.

Things happen very quickly in skiing. In a matter of seconds you may have to make a sudden movement to avoid a fall, or a collision with another skier or object in your path.

Flexible muscles also reduce chances of severe injury. You may be in a situation where you suddenly catch the tip of a ski in the snow. Your direction of fall may place a sudden and severe pulling force on the muscles in the back of the calf, knee, or thigh. Being flexible is no guarantee that you won't sustain muscle pulls, but it's less likely that you'll suffer serious damage to the muscles.

When you ski, you never want to lock yourself into any one body position. You'll always be moving, changing positions, shifting weight, and turning the skis. You want to feel what the slope does to you as you pass over it. Relax, glide along. Let yourself go. If you try to prevent the forward sliding of your skis over the snow, then you're not skiing. When your muscles are flexible you will feel lighter and be able to move with less effort.

Flexibility is one of the keys to feeling well every day in all daily activities, not just on the slope. In fact, neck aches and backaches are frequently linked to tight, shortened muscles, often the result of the emotional stress in daily living. If you're looking for a year-round bonus, increase your flexibility. You will be taking a very significant step toward counteracting the strain and muscle tension that is such a common problem in today's society.

In addition to strength and flexibility, a skier needs endurance. To have endurance is to have the ability to do vigorous work over and over again. The work activity itself may not be strenuous or difficult, but to do it repeatedly makes it vigorous. Endurance also refers to the ability of your heart and lungs to sustain your level of activity. To get better at what you're doing on skis you have to put in miles and miles of practice. You'll want the stamina to be able to ski down, ride the lift up, and go down and up many times a day. Some ski instructors suggest that skiing skills improve faster if you don't keep stopping. With the endurance to ski many runs in a day you'll develop a feeling for the flow and motion of continuous skiing.

Skiing is a great sport, but it's also a physically demanding one. Always keep one thing in mind. Your primary goal should be your own enjoyment. The purpose of this book is to help you to get into better shape so that you can enjoy skiing more. You don't have to be as good as anyone else or better than anyone else in order to benefit from these exercises or from participating in this sport. Recreational skiing can be anything you want it to be.

2 || A Close Look at Downhill Skiing

The exercises recommended in this book cover stretching for flexibility, isometric (holding) and isotonic (active) muscular contractions for strength, and endurance exercises for stamina. These exercises relate very specifically to things you will be doing repeatedly throughout a day on the slopes. Some are for increasing your body's awareness and sensitivity to the feel of different positions, and some are exercises for agility.

To get a clearer picture of the demands made on a skier and a better understanding of the forces which come into play, let's follow a new skier for a day, assuming that he starts out as a beginner and gets very good very quickly. In fact, in one day-long, magical run he goes from beginner to expert. If we watch very carefully we may notice that although his techniques change, many of his body movements are repeated over and over again even though he is getting to be a better skier all the time.

Our skier is getting off the lift at the top of a long slope. It's cold, in fact he's cold and stiff and maybe not as anxious to point his skis downhill as he expected to be when he was sitting in the lodge a few minutes ago. Well, here he goes, hands high, knees locked, snowplowing with all his might! He is now traveling downhill at about two miles per hour! All his muscles are tensed. He's not cold anymore. After a few hundred feet our fast learner realizes that he had better improve. He relaxes a bit, bends his knees and steers his skis by using his inside edges. His knees roll inward, his legs push the tails of the skis outward, and he shifts his weight down onto the outside ski of the turn with a sinking motion of both knees. That's more like it! With new confidence off he goes again down the slope.

This time he's in a straight running position with the skis about shoulder width apart, his body erect but with a comfortable bend at the hips, knees, and ankles. He's more resilient now, letting his legs fold up and down underneath him as the skis pass over some very small bumps and ridges. He lets his legs act as shock absorbers for the fluctuations in the snow surface and keeps the rest of his body loose and balanced. He feels ready to be able to shift his weight a bit further forward or backward as he rides over some larger bumps, still absorbing the terrain with his legs. He's becoming so good at shifting his weight from one side to the other that he can lift one ski off of the snow entirely while continuing to travel forward.

He begins to pick up a little too much speed for the narrow path he's approaching; so he slows down with the snowplow position. He gains stability by spreading the skis out in a side "V". All the time that he stays in this wedge position, his knees are partially bent while they are also rolled inward to keep both skis on their inside edges.

The trail opens up considerably, and the

Snowplow

Straight run

Snowplow turn

Terrain absorbtion

skier's run continues with the skis moving slightly closer together, parallel to each other. The slope pitches a bit more, and he decides to try some stem turns. Traveling across the slope for a distance with the skis parallel, he spreads the uphill out to the side to form half of a wedge. This ski is riding on its inner edge when the knee rolls inward. He shifts most of his weight onto the ski, the skis both round the turn, and his body stays low. As the turn is completed, the skier rises up a little, the skis slide together, and he continues across the slope.

He's ready to make a turn to the opposite direction; well, almost ready. It appears that our Super Skier has crossed his tips and for the moment is lying on his back after a sudden but not serious fall. His next problem is to get back on his feet again and then recover his hat which is about twenty feet up the hill. Step number one is to untangle himself and get his skis next to one another, aligned across the hill and downhill from his body. His second step is to keep the skis on their uphill edges as he gets up to keep them from sliding downward. As he pushes himself up, he keeps his knees rolled toward the hill to maintain the edging action. And so he's ready to start the climb up to get his hat.

Walking uphill is another adventure. He

Herringbone

rolled in toward the hill. To compensate for the lower body angling in toward the hill he bends his upper body away from the hill to keep his edging, stepping and balance in progress. Hat on, a few minutes to catch his breath and he's off again, this time making some uninterrupted, linked stem turns.

Remembering everything that he ever read about ski technique, he attempts some parallel turns using "down-weighting." For these, he heads more directly down the fall line rather than starting from a traverse. He makes turns with a fairly short radius and changes the edges of both skis simultaneously. He finds that he can use a little rebound from one turn to help start his next turn. He uses this rebound to lift the skis ever so slightly from the snow, unweighting them for a brief moment so that he can easily position his legs to come down on the skis' turning edges. For the rebound to occur, he finds that he must bend his knees when he plants his pole and then let the power from his legs extend them slightly until he lowers again for the following edge set. In this way he continues downhill with the skis moving across from right to left over and over again.

The skier is doing very nicely now, but finds himself skiing on snow that is more unpredictable than before. The surface has some icy patches and so our skier decides that he would feel more secure if he could keep his skis more consistently in contact with the snow. This can be accomplished by using a technique known as "down-unweighting." For these turns he quickly lowers his hips as he starts the turn and takes advantage of the very short interval during this lowering to change edges and direction. As he does this, he's reminded of the feeling of weightlessness he gets when he rides an elevator and it suddenly starts to descend.

His turns are faster and faster, and it's plenty of hard work. He's beginning to tire. Fortunately, there's a stretch ahead that he can

starts by using a "herringbone" step, which is essentially walking straight up the hill with the skis spread out in a "V" pointing downhill. He moves about five feet and then realizes that on such a steep slope side stepping his way up will be less tiring and just as efficient.

He faces across the hill, skis parallel. This time he steps each ski uphill, as if he's walking up a flight of stairs sideways. Each step of the uphill leg moves the ski sideways from the body, and each step of the downhill leg moves that ski in toward the center of the body. To keep from sliding down the slope, his knees are

Anticipation

schuss; head down, elbows tucked with the poles under his armpits, he cruises straight down the hill.

The bottom of the slope is in sight, but before he's actually there he has to negotiate some big, steep moguls. They are too large and irregular to ride up and over just by letting the bump flex his legs. He slides around them from one trough to the next, but finds that the skis skid too much and he can't keep his speed under control. Finally, he tries to turn on the top of each mogul where the snow is more plentiful and better for turning. He approaches each bump, plants his pole downhill, and anticipates the turn by fac-

ing his upper body in the direction of the fall line although his skis are still pointing across the hill. The upper body twist proves to be very useful. A few more of these, another straight tuck to the bottom, and a strong parallel stop for all the folks in the lift line. Not a bad first run!

We have just seen a display of ski technique from beginner to expert. Now, let's take another look at our skier's run, but this time let's focus on specific body motions with emphasis on those which are frequently repeated. This will help you to see the importance of doing a wide variety of exercises in preparing yourself for the range of physical demands that you experience as a skier.

At all times, our skier tried to maintain a comfortable stance on his skis with his joints slightly flexed. This put him in a position of readiness, able to move easily in any direction. He was using his head, neck, stomach, and back muscles for continuous, subtle adjustments in balance. In these regions of the body the skier needed freedom of motion and flexibility to move quickly, especially when the shoulder and hips twisted in opposing directions.

He used upper arms, shoulder girdle, and back muscles to push up from the ground when he fell, to assist in walking uphill with the herringbone step, or anytime that he had to pole hard on flat surfaces.

Whether traversing, climbing, turning, or straight running, his knees were bent most of the time. This put constant stress on the muscles in the front of the thigh that control the amount of knee bending. When he used leg power to push up as in up-unweighting, a motion similar to the everyday motions of jumping and climbing, he used muscles in the front of the thigh, calves, buttocks, and back. Muscles in the front of the chest and upper and lower arms also participated in the poling action during turns.

When our skier did his parallel turns with a down motion to unweight, he used muscles in quite a different way. His rapid motion downward utilized muscles more in the abdomen, front of the hip joints, back of the thighs, and front of the lower leg.

At various times our skier moved his skis apart and together. This involved use of muscles in the outer and inner hip and thighs. When he shifted his body weight from one leg to the other and balanced with most of his body weight over one ski, he was placing a strong isometric workload on muscles around the pelvis and hips.

We saw our skier make several types of turns from beginner to advanced, all with the same purpose: to steer the skis. All involved the same leg function: applying pressure to the turning ski that was placed on edge. Skiers are encouraged to edge their skis by being reminded to "roll their knees into the hill," "angulate the knees," or by "pushing their knees hard into the hill." No matter which description you may have heard, they all amount to the same thing; that the knees are bent and displaced to one side or the other to "set" the ski edges into the snow.

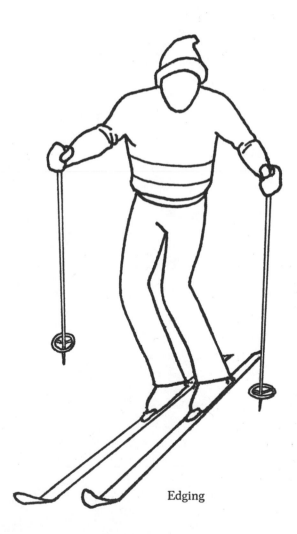

Edging

It's important to understand this mechanism in more detail because it points out the uniqueness of the ski position. First of all, the knee is a hinge type of joint capable of motion in only two directions: bending and straightening. When the knee is seen to move in a rolling motion to the side, the actual motion is produced by rotation of the thigh bone in the socket of the hip joint. So, what we really have is a sideward and rotary movement of the thigh bone (femur) in the hip socket which gives the knee the appearance of rolling from side to side. What is especially significant for ski condition-ing is that this rotary motion of the upper leg is not common in our usual daily activities. Consequently, the power to produce this movement is poorly developed in most people.

In general, developing a flexible body that can move quickly without strain and a strong body that can sustain a skier in the positions needed to execute maneuvers serves as the best basic prescription for skiing preparation. Remember also that these same qualities make it easier for you to regain your balance if you are on the verge of a fall and reduce the chance of serious injury if a fall can't be avoided.

3 | A Close Look at Cross-Country Skiing

To the casual, uninitiated observer there appear to be some strong similarities between downhill and cross-country skiing. After all, both are done on the snow using skis, boots, and poles, and the participants are men, women, and children of all ages. From this one might assume that they are very similar sports. Each requires the skier to have good physical strength, flexibility, and endurance, but the specifics of these requirements differ quite a bit, as we will see.

Cross-country skiing is a lot like walking, except that it takes more energy. Still, it offers some distinct advantages for older people whose joints can't take the constant stress of downhill maneuvering. There is little stress on the hip and knee joints, affording excellent exercise even for skiers with mild arthritis. For the diagonal stride on flat surfaces you kick and glide the legs past each other, reciprocally swing the arms forward and push to the rear, and alternate the feet from flat to push-off.

Good cross-country skiing has smooth, flowing, continuous motion. The rhythmical use of large masses of muscle that alternately contract and relax promote a healthy stimulation to the muscular system, heart, and general circulation. The intervals of muscular rest are known as "micro pauses." There are none of the isometric, "holding" movements so frequent in

Diagonal stride

downhill skiing. This is another factor that makes cross-country so suitable for older skiers who should avoid the prolonged tension of muscles that impedes the natural flow of blood through the muscle tissue. The cross-country skier is more apt to feel pleasantly fatigued overall, rather than in specific muscles such as is frequently experienced in the thighs of the downhiller who supports his weight with bent knees for long periods of time. Muscular aches and pains are relatively uncommon, as are severe injuries, although the unconditioned skier can develop muscular soreness particularly in the calves, upper arms, and abdominal muscles.

Leg power in cross-country comes from two phases of the stride. Your leg kicks down and back, followed by a driving motion forward. The more strength you have in both directions, the faster and more efficient you will be. A strong kick on the flat straightens your leg behind you. In this motion, muscles in the front of the hip and thigh are stretched, while those in the buttock and back of the thigh and calf work hard for the force and acceleration. On very steep inclines you may take your stride with a straighter knee and use more power from the buttock muscles to get you up the hill. Remember, although your arms are there for stabilizing and balancing, it is the legs that provide the main power supply for getting uphill.

To drive your leg forward in the second phase of the stride, muscles in the front of the hip work vigorously while those in the buttock are now put on stretch. To take long strides and bound up hills takes ample ankle flexibility to help cushion the forward-rolling motion of your body. Without strength and speed in the kick, you can't expect to ski smoothly and quickly. When using the diagonal stride up hills you really need extra glide, drive, and push. If you use a herringbone climb uphill, good hip and ankle flexibility make the climb easier.

Good shoulder flexibility, both forward and backward, enables you to swing each arm fully for momentum and good body alignment. Sufficient strength in muscles above the elbow and in the forearm provide power for pushing down and backward and for re-grasping the pole at the start of the next swing forward. With speed, the diagonal stride pattern turns the trunk slightly, but if you have a stiff and tight middle and lower back your body won't tolerate this slight rotation very well.

Poling with both arms simultaneously (double poling) calls for work in the abdominal muscles. You can get a feel for this action if you sit at a table and place both hands on top of it. If you then try to push your hands downward through the table, you can immediately feel the tension built up in the abdominal muscles.

Whether you like to go it alone and make your own tracks in the snow or follow in the path of another skier, cross-country can't be beat as an activity that requires good endurance. It rates very highly as an aerobic activity; that is, it provides a sustained demand on your heart and lungs to deliver an adequate supply of oxygen to your body. With aerobic capacity as one very important aspect of physical fitness, competitive cross-country skiers rank among the most physically fit athletes in the world.

To summarize: The areas of conditioning emphasis for cross-country skiers are

1. Flexibility of hip joints, shoulder joints, and lower back.
2. Strength in hip flexion and extension, foot plantar flexion, abdominal flexion, and elbow extension.
3. Aerobic conditioning for heart and lungs.

If cross-country skiing is your sport, keep these regions of the body in mind when you are planning your Basic Program. Remember that any muscular region that you develop for strength must also be treated to stretching exercises.

THE CROSS-COUNTRY SKIER'S "TENNIS ELBOW"

Elbow pain in cross-country skiers may be produced by the same type of muscular stress that causes the more well-known syndrome, "tennis elbow." Repeated grasping of the ski pole stresses forearm muscles near the elbow in a way that may create a minor irritation of the tendons in that area. The discomfort is similar, but usually less severe, than that of the tennis player's.

The immediate remedy is to stop repeating the motion that causes the tendon irritation; so stop skiing and give it plenty of rest from poling. See your doctor if the discomfort persists. Very importantly, follow a program of tennis elbow exercises to give these muscles the added protection of additional strength before you ski again. If you go back to poling too soon, before the irritation has completely subsided, you are making it more difficult for healing to proceed quickly and fully.

There are so many skiers who are also tennis players that the program of tennis elbow exercises is included in this book (see Appendix D) for all those who have had this problem with tennis or skiing. (In tennis, the mechanism of stress on the extensor tendons comes from trying to flick the wrist backward instead of leading from the shoulder in the backhand stroke. Other contributing factors are a racket that is too heavy, strung too tightly, a grip that is too small, or a backhand stroke giving top spin to the ball by rapidly rotating the forearm).

4 || Muscles and Movements

To understand the work of our muscles in skiing, we first have to understand some basic concepts about the structure and mechanical functioning of the muscular system.

The body has several different types of muscle tissue: smooth muscle, found, for example, in the digestive tract; cardiac muscle, found in the heart; and striated or voluntary muscle, the "meat" around our bones. Voluntary muscle, which moves the parts of our bony skeleton, is the type that will be discussed here. Let's simply call them skeletal muscles.

Each skeletal muscle is able to undergo shortening or contraction, which occurs when the muscle receives an impulse to contract from its nerve supply. Under normal conditions, a skeletal muscle cannot contract unless it receives a nerve impulse. The nerve supply has "motor" fibers to carry signals to the muscle to stimulate it to contract and from the muscular area via "sensory" fibers to relay information such as pain from aching muscles to the central nervous system. Other nerve fibers called proprioceptive fibers transmit information concerning the length and the state of contraction or tension within a muscle. Most of these information relays occur on a subconscious level. If muscular activity is to be smooth and coordinated, it must always "know" just how to react to the body's needs at that instant.

Each whole muscle is made up of individual filaments called myofilaments, which overlap and come closer together when the muscle contracts. For this to happen the myofilaments must have an energy source. This source is a substance know as ATP (adenosinetriphosphate). ATP is formed when glucose stored in small quantity in the muscles and in the liver is oxidized. But in instances where there isn't enough oxygen available, as in strenuous exercise, the glucose is converted to lactic acid, which accumulates in the muscle. This need for more oxygen than is available at the moment is called "oxygen debt." This is what happens when you are skiing, your thighs develop the sensation of extreme fatigue and burning, and you are breathing very rapidly. When you stop to rest and catch your breath the "oxygen debt" is repaid to the system; glucose is reformed, lactic acid is metabolized, and the moment of temporary exhaustion passes.

Good physical fitness in the cardio-respiratory system (heart, blood vessels, and lungs) through endurance training has a large influence on the body's ability to take in and utilize oxygen well, use glucose, and delay the formation of lactic acid. This is what endurance training is all about: training the body to function efficiently without creating an oxygen "debt." When the energy supply to the muscles works better, the muscles themselves are better nourished and their effort is improved.

The strength of a muscle is a different story. Strength depends on the number and size of its fibers. No amount of exercise will increase the number of fibers in a muscle. Increases in size and strength of the whole muscle are an increase in the size of each individual fiber.

The reason muscles require energy and undergo contraction is to move the bones of the skeleton. A typical muscle is attached at each of its ends to bone, and it spans over one or two joints. When the muscle contracts and shortens it moves bone toward bone. In many muscles the fibers that attach directly to the bone are strong, tough fibers called tendons. Tendonous attachments allow a bulky muscle such as in the calf to be attached to a relatively small area of bone such as at the heel. (This is what is commonly known as the heel cord or Achilles tendon.) Also, the muscles of the forearm insert as thin tendons into the bones of the wrist and hand.

When the muscle shortens in length and causes the bony part to move it is called an "isotonic" contraction, referred to in the text as isotonic or active movements. If an opposing muscle located on the opposite side of the joint contracts with an equal amount of tension, neither muscle shortens and no movement occurs although the muscles develop tension. This is called an "isometric" contraction, referred to in the text as isometric or holding contractions.

Muscles work in yet another way. Some movements arc carried out by gravity; knee bending is one example. When you stand, the role of the muscles is to prevent the knees from succumbing totally to gravity and buckling. This requires controlled muscular *lengthening* and is called an "eccentric" contraction. When skiing, this is the mechanism that is in play in the front of the thigh all the time that your knees are bent, which should be all of the time.

When a muscle isn't given the opportunity to stretch over its full length it gradually loses its ability to do so. Progressively it adapts to the shorter length and with time becomes more and more difficult to elongate completely. The normal aging process which reduces the elasticity of muscle fibers and the smoothness of joint motions makes it essential for people to do stretching and flexibility exercises throughout life.

If you follow an exercise program that works only on muscular strengthening and ignores the stretching aspect altogether, you're asking for trouble. You need to provide your muscular system with a balanced dose of stretching and strengthening. Muscles that are too short and tight lose their ability to elongate fully. If a sudden stretch does occur while skiing, this very tight muscle may not be able to yield and the result is a muscle pull or muscle tear.

The whole musculo-skeletal system works so much better when the muscles can contract, stretch, and relax. Relaxation is extremely important. If muscular fibers are under tension too much of the time without a rest period, they adapt to the pre-tensed state and become less effective for contraction. The best contractions are usually preceded by some degree of stretch.

Muscles rarely work alone. Movements of the body are usually produced by the coordinated action of several muscles working as a group. The regions of the body delineated for the Basic Program represent groups of muscles working together to produce certain body motions. The human body is capable of a wide range of movement combinations because of the interplay of the muscular system.

At times, muscle groups around a joint all contract simultaneously. At other times, one group contracts while the other relaxes or only partially contracts. The amount and direction of movement that is possible is determined by the type of joint connecting the bony parts. The force and speed of the movement is determined by the actions of the muscles crossing the joint. Ligaments, tough, fibrous bands attached over short distances from bone to bone, also help to guide and limit the amount of movement allowed at a joint.

5 || Planning a Skier's Exercise Program

In the first few chapters we have tried to emphasize that although skiing can mean different things to different people, it has one characteristic that will take a lot of our attention: that it can be a very physically demanding sport. Let's review for a moment what some of these demands are. The well prepared skier needs muscular strength and flexibility as well as cardio-respiratory endurance to get the most enjoyment and to enhance his performance.

Although we may often ski at a fast speed, the muscular system frequently works in a slow, holding way to stabilize and balance the skier over his skis. The muscular system also needs flexibility to absorb changes in the terrain as well as the stresses that falling places on the body. A skier needs the energy to ski several hours a day without excessive fatigue.

The exercises that you do to fulfill the requirements of ski conditioning must be suitable to the sport, and, most importantly, suitable to your needs. You may be a fairly good skier but you may not be an athlete. And if, like most recreational skiers, you are a "weekend athlete" you have tight muscles all during the week, put them through great stress on the weekend thinking that you can ski yourself into good shape, and then find that you're tight again all during the following week. Even if you consider yourself to be athletic, you may have muscular imbalances that make you more susceptible to sports-related injuries such as pulled muscles.

We have different needs because some of us are more naturally tight-jointed or loose-jointed than others.

Your exercise program should allow you to begin at a level that does not overtax your abilities at the start. It should enable you to progress at your own rate and provide progressive exercises for you to work up to as your physical condition improves. That is why you will see many exercises in this book that are presented in both easy and more advanced versions. A good exercise program always includes a warming-up and a cooling-down phase. These, too, you will find in this book's Basic Program.

Ideally, you should enjoy the exercises that you do. If not, there is a strong likelihood that you'll get bored and give them up. You will be reminded throughout this book to do only the exercises that you are ready for. If you attempt to do exercises that are too difficult you will not only become easily discouraged, but you may injure yourself to the point where you have to temporarily discontinue exercising altogether. Remember it took a while to get out of shape and it will take time to get into condition again.

In this book you will find several exercises for the same purpose; either to stretch or strengthen a particular muscular region of the body. The differences between them are that they can be done from a variety of positions. In this program you can find the position that gives you the best enjoyment for your time spent in exercising. In any case, *you must exercise regularly. If you do not, then whatever time you do spend on exercising is wasted time. If you don't intend to do it properly, then do yourself a favor and don't start at all.*

PLANNING AN EXERCISE PROGRAM

The first step in planning your own program is determining your level of physical fitness. To help you evaluate yourself you must take the brief Physical Fitness Quiz in Chapter 9. The first part of the quiz, tests 1 through 6, consists of test positions from the Kraus-Weber Tests for Minimum Physical Fitness. In these tests you are checking the minimum strength and flexibility of key postural muscles that are essential for healthy living. The tests are designed to see if you have sufficient strength and flexibility for your own size and weight.

Dr. Hans Kraus, a prominent physician and co-author of the tests, stresses that the tests are indicators of minimum levels of fitness and that even completing them all in good form may not constitute adequate fitness levels. On the other hand, Dr. Kraus has found that there is a correlation between people who have difficulty with these tests and people who are prone to

chronic back pain, neckache, or other tension-related muscular problems. In most cases, the chief cause of these problems is under-exercise. A common physical profile of someone in this category is one who has insufficient abdominal strength and/or insufficient back extensor and hamstring flexibility. If you fail or have difficulty with any part of the quiz, refer to the corrective exercises specified at the end of each test. In this book, exercises are arranged by regions of the body so that you can easily locate the different areas.

The corrective exercises must be incorporated into your Basic Program. For the first month or so of exercising you may be doing *only* remedial exercises. That's perfectly all right. You're doing exactly what you need to do for your individual needs. From this foundation you can build yourself up and add other exercises. Some skiers may be doing some corrective exercises and some of the other standard exercises from the very beginning. That's fine, too. You just have to do whatever is necessary for you to do to derive the most benefit.

The second part of the quiz focuses on areas of fitness more closely related to skiing. Muscles which require particularly good strength for skiing or muscles that are subjected to sudden stretches will be tested. Here too, corrective exercises will be suggested for those tests where you find you're not quite up to par.

6 | Introduction to the Basic Program

Exercising must be regular, but it doesn't have to be rigid and boring. The Skier's Year-Round Exercise Program allows you to design a program for every day of the year that combines sound physical conditioning with variety and interest. Getting into good physical condition and staying that way is easy if you know exactly what to do.

You start by taking the Physical Fitness Quiz. Your progress in exercising depends a lot on an honest assessment of your starting level of fitness. You are cheating and possibly harming yourself if you attempt to do exercises that you think are good for you or that you think you should be doing, but that, in reality, are too difficult for you. You'll be more satisfied with yourself and with your improvements if you go at a reasonable pace, consistent with your personal needs.

The Basic Program consists of exercises arranged by regions of the body, eleven regions in all as seen in the full body diagrams. Within each region you will find two categories of exercise: one for stretching and the other for strengthening.

In the beginning of each region you will find a section for *Anatomy* and *Function*. The Anatomy section tells you the approximate location of the muscle or muscles of the region, the movement or movements that result when the muscle contracts, and the range of movement that occurs with normal flexibility. Look at the anatomical illustrations that appear in the beginning of each region. The arrows show you the direction of possible movements for that region. Strengthening exercises will have you move in the direction of the arrow. Motion in this direction contracts the muscle or muscles being considered. Stretching exercises will have you move in the direction opposite to the arrow. Moving in this direction elongates the muscle.

For example, the movement of hip flexion, p. 104, brings the thigh toward the torso. Therefore, strengthening exercises for this movement involve positions that have your thigh move in the direction of the flexion arrow. Exercises 47 and 48 have this type of motion.

Stretching exercises for hip flexion involve positions that move the thigh away from the torso, opposite to the flexion arrow. Exercises 42 and 43 have this type of motion.

In some places the names of muscles have been added to help clarify your understanding of the location and function of some of the most commonly known muscles.

The section on Function gives you specific information about the ski positions that use the muscles of the region.

In most regions you will find some type of Special Instructions. They may pertain to exercises that you must do if you failed any tests on the Physical Fitness Quiz. Or, they may pertain to specific characteristics of that particular region of the body. Read all of these instructions

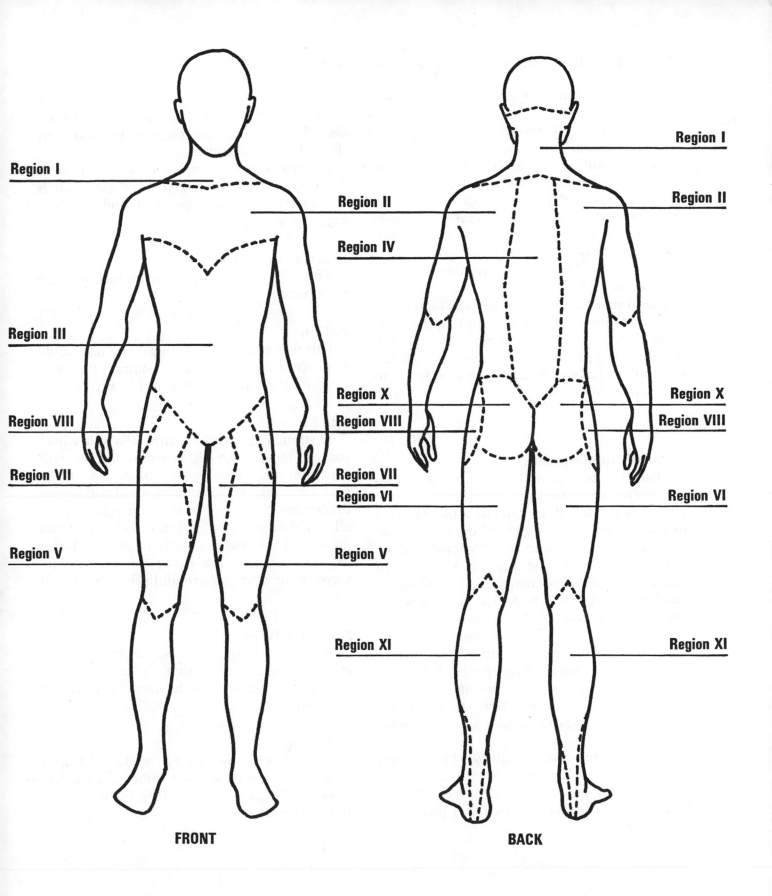

FRONT

BACK

Region I

Region I

Region II

Region II

Region IV

Region III

Region X

Region VIII

Region VII

Region VI

Region V

Region X

Region VIII

Region VII

Region VI

Region V

Region XI

Region XI

carefully to derive the greatest benefit from your exercise program.

Each exercise is presented in a standard form. The information given with each exercise is very important, and you should read it completely before any exercise is practiced for the first time. Even if you recognize the exercise from its illustration and know that you've done it before, please read the accompanying information. Much of the information provided with each exercise is not usually available in other exercise books.

The format for each exercise is as follows: The solid lines indicate the starting position. Dotted lines and arrows indicate the position and direction of the exercise movement. Some illustrations have more than one solid figure to show the movements.

Name of the Exercise

This may be followed by the word "remedial." This indicates that the exercise is compulsory if you failed the Quiz item that pertains to that region and category of the body. However, this does not mean that it should be done only by those who need remedial exercises. In many instances, particularly in the abdominal muscle region, the "remedial" exercises are highly recommended for everyone.

"Limbering" movements are used as a warm-up to prepare the muscles and joints and take them through an easy mobility pattern before you start more vigorous movements. "Limbering"exercises are not something that you outgrow. They are an essential part of every exercise session.

The name may also be followed by the word "isometric." This indicates that it is a strengthening exercise of the holding variety. That is, tension is created in the muscle, but there is no movement of the body parts. If the word "isotonic" is seen, it refers to strengthening exercises that create muscular tension but also allow the body parts to move.

In some cases the name of the exercise is descriptive. It will tell you the region that is being stretched or strengthened, and the starting position.

Starting Position

This tells you what position to take to begin the exercise.

Action

This tells you what movement you have to do to produce the stretch or to contract the muscle(s) for the standard form of the exercise.

The Stretch

In stretching exercises, this tells you where you will feel the stretching sensation. This will vary somewhat from person to person due to each individual's different degree of stiffness or limberness. You may feel the stretch in some or all of the areas listed. If you discover that you do not feel the stretch sensations as described it may be that you are doing the exercise incorrectly or that you are quite flexible in that area.

Muscular Work

In strengthening exercises, this tells you the location of the muscles that are contracting to produce the tension or the movement of the exercise.

Progression

This tells you how to vary the standard form to make the exercise more difficult. In a few cases, the progression will tell you how to make an exercise easier.

Variation

This tells you of other ways to perform the exercise without making it more or less difficult.

Comments

This section is reserved for suggestions pertaining to your performance of the exercise. It tells you how to avoid the common mistakes that are made in performing that exercise and which exercises to avoid in the presence of certain orthopedic problems.

The Basic Program emphasizes the muscles and movements most frequently stressed in skiing and in everyday activities. Additional movements and exercises are given in the chapter on rehabilitation. If you have unusual stiffness or weakness related or unrelated to a specific recent or past injury, you can refer to the rehabilitation section for supplemental exercises that you would like to do in your Basic Program.

The program is designed to be done at home with a minimum of exercise equipment. Take the time to plan your Basic Program. You'll be able to get much more benefit from a program that appeals to you because you'll be more likely to exercise regularly. Design a program that has variety and that makes *you* feel good. For each exercise you should be able to answer the question, "What is the purpose of this exercise?" When you have a good idea of *what* you are doing, not only *how* to do it, you are on the way to exercising that is easier with results that come faster.

7 || How to Create Your Own Basic Program

Step 1 Take the Physical Fitness Quiz. Record the results on your Physical Fitness Quiz Recording Sheet.

Step 2 *If you failed one or more of the tests:* Refer to the appropriate body region for the tests that you failed. In each region where remedial exercises appear they are designated "remedial." Check these off on your Basic Program Planning Chart in the "Initial" column. To complete the remainder of your plan sheet, go through the book region by region. Read the *Special Instructions* that appear with each region to determine which exercises you will need for your Initial Program. In some cases they will tell you to do more than one exercise from that region. Check off the exercises you plan to do in the "Initial" column. Learn and stick to your initial program. This gives you a foundation on which to build. After several weeks or after your first re-evaluation, you can start to make changes in your program.

 If you passed all of the tests: Look through the exercises in each region, again following the *Special Instructions* to complete your program for all eleven regions. Check off the exercises you pick to do in the "Initial" column. You need not avoid exercises designated as "remedial." These are excellent basic exercises done alone or as brief warm-ups for more strenuous exercises.

Step 3 Review the exercises that you have written on your plan sheet for your first Basic Program. Be sure that you have included at least one from each category in each region as instructed. It's common to have easier exercises for some regions of the body and more advanced exercises for other regions. In some regions you will see exercises that are designated "isometric." These are the holding contractions. Again, the *Special Instructions* will tell you to pick one of these in addition to your regular strengthening exercise.

Step 4 Take a few minutes to make sure that your exercise plan is complete. The time that you spend will save you many wasted minutes later on, when you are trying to recall things from memory, or searching for the page to re-read an exercise or check an illustration.

Step 5 Read the Guidelines for Stretching Exercises and Guidelines for Strengthening Exercises in the next chapter.

Step 6 Read the complete instructions for each exercise before you start to do it. Until you are totally familiar with the exercise, refer frequently to the book to double-check that you are doing it exactly as it is written in the book. Start and end each exercise session with limbering exercises to provide a warm-up and a cool-down period. It is very important to prepare your muscles for the work of exercising and to treat them well after a workout. The more out of condition or the older you are, the more time you should devote to limbering.

After you do your limbering exercises, next do leg exercises, from regions V through XI. This takes advantage of the pumping action that the leg muscles provide for your blood circulation and helps ready your body for vigorous exercise.

Other than doing the leg exercises first, the precise order of the exercises is not important. It is advantageous to stretch a region just before you do the strengthening for it. Or, you can do one repetition of the stretch, follow with the strengthening repetitions and then repeat one repetition of the stretch. Remember, if you try to exercise only for development of strength, you are constantly shortening your muscles without giving them the opportunity for full elongation. Too much shortening without adequate stretching makes the muscles less tolerant to sudden stress and strain.

Older skiers should avoid the isometric strengthening contractions, as there is a tendency for people to hold their breath and strain themselves throughout the tensing phase. Instead, they should concentrate on easy, rhythmical, active movements.

Incorporate any of the intermittent relaxation exercises at any time during your exercise session.

Always do specific stretches for all parts of the legs before you do any endurance training such as jogging, running, jumping rope or bench jumps which require powerful, repetitive leg work.

Step 7 After a few weeks you will be ready to make some changes in your Basic Program. Your body will tell you it has accommodated to the stretches, for they will become easier to do. Strengthening exercises will be easier and you will be able to do many more repetitions without fatigue. Always start any new exercise with the easiest form and progress to the more difficult. *Variations* written after an exercise indicates that these are slightly different methods for achieving the same result. Use them for variety. In most cases, they are no harder or easier than the standard form of the exercise. *Progressions* written after an exercise indicates a version of the exercise that is significantly harder or easier. Add or modify exercises one at a time so that your Basic Program doesn't change drastically from one day to the next.

It's more important to do exercises properly even if they are easy than to attempt forms that are too tough and to execute them in poor form.

Use the Repetitions/Weight column 4 on your plan sheet to keep a record of the number of repetitions and/or the amount of weight you use in strengthening exercises. Retest yourself every 4 weeks on Fitness Quiz tests that you have failed or scored poorly on. Use the 4-week and 8-week columns to check off the exercises that you add or revise as you modify your Basic Program.

8 || Ground Rules for Exercising

1. Set time aside to exercise when you won't be rushed or interrupted. It is ideal to have a specified time set aside each day.

2. Exercises must be done on a regular basis if you are to see results. Doing exercises sporadically can be more harmful than not doing them at all. If you must stop, remember when you begin again to go easy. Always do easier forms of the exercises until you are comfortably back to your previous level.

3. Don't make excuses such as "I'm too tired" or "I'm too busy." Frequently, these are the times when exercising will benefit you the most, helping you to relax, restore your energy, and release tension. Make a special effort to exercise on these days. Limbering and relaxation exercises can really help you unwind at the end of a hectic day.

4. Do the stretching exercises in your program daily.

   Do the strengthening exercises in your program no less than 3 times a week (not on 3 consecutive days).

   If you are working on remedial exercises for strengthening, do them daily also.

5. Wear comfortable clothing that is loose and allows you to move freely.

6. Perform the movements slowly and smoothly.

You don't use jerky motions when you ski, so neither should you use them when you exercise. Rest a few moments between each exercise.

7. If you find it helpful, use music to help you establish a comfortable pace and rhythm.

8. Make a list of your exercises and keep it where it can be seen for reference when you exercise. Or, record the instructions for each of your exercises on a tape and play it back for yourself as you exercise.

9. Do floor exercises on a well-padded mat or soft rug. The surface should be firm but not unbearably hard.

10. If you have a cold or other illness, don't try to "work it out" by exercising vigorously. You're much better off discontinuing exercising until your health is improved. You can try to do some easy stretching if you're in bed to reduce some of the stiffness you feel from lack of normal activity.

11. Don't exercise immediately after eating.

12. Don't compare yourself with anyone else. Your program and your progress are highly individualized. Remember that your performance may be slightly different from day to day, but this is normal.

13. Check with your doctor before starting your exercise program.

GUIDELINES FOR STRETCHING EXERCISES

1. Go easy, easy, easy. Try to make progress that is gradual, and you will find that you'll make forward progress. It took time for your muscles to become tight, and it will take time to elongate them again. Once you begin to work regularly at stretching you'll see how quickly your muscles adapt to the longer length. You have to continue to do stretching to maintain your improvement. You'll feel better, look better, and move better when regular stretching becomes a part of your life.

2. Each exercise tells you where you should feel the stretching sensation. You may not feel a stretch in all of the places listed. If you are extraordinarily flexible you may not feel the stretch intensely, but you should still perform the exercises to maintain your good mobility, particularly if you are young.

Once you feel the proper stretch, hold the position for the specified number of seconds. You may stretch longer than the time given, but do not stretch for a shorter duration. Make sure that you are relaxed. This means that you should continue to breathe in a normal manner. Never hold your breath.

Gradually build up to the specified number of seconds over a period of days or weeks if you cannot do it initially. It doesn't matter how long it takes you to build up your tolerance. Be consistent and regular in your exercising, and you will see improvements.

3. Move into each stretching position in a way that is slow, smooth, and controlled. Don't bounce. Bouncing can elicit a stretch reflex that causes your muscle to contract rather than stretch. Bouncing may cause you to stretch your muscles beyond a safe range, because you have less control over the excursion of the movement.

4. Stretching is personal. You will have to feel for yourself what a good, beneficial pulling sensation feels like. Stretching should never be painful. If it is, then you are trying to do too much. Good stretching is done in a relaxed way within your own limits.

5. Look for opportunities to do stretches throughout the day. Refer to the chapter on Mini-exercises for suggestions on daily stretches in addition to your Basic Program. Stretching becomes addictive once you discover how good your body feels. You'll want to find ways to do it whenever you start to feel some tension developing in your body. You'll find this particularly helpful for muscles of the neck and shoulders if you've been working over a desk for a long time, driving a car for a long period of time, or for muscle tension due to anxiety or stress.

6. Doing stretching exercises makes you more aware of the different kinds of feelings your body has that differentiate tension from relaxation.

GUIDELINES FOR STRENGTHENING EXERCISES

1. Perform the movements slowly, smoothly, and exactly as instructed. Rest a few moments in between different strengthening exercises.

2. Do not hold your breath! Breathe normally. Counting out loud is one way to keep yourself breathing throughout the exercise. For some exercises you will have specific instructions when

to inhale and when to exhale with the movements.

3. Start with 3 or 4 repetitions of each strengthening exercise and gradually work up to 15 repetitions. In instances where special instructions are given concerning the number of repetitions, follow them carefully.

4. The *action* part of a strengthening exercise should be completed in 2 to 3 seconds. The return movement to the starting position should take about twice as long as the action. For example, when doing a full sit-up, use 2 counts to come up and 4 counts to return to the floor.

5. Strengthening exercises are isotonic (muscular tension with the body part moving) unless specifically designated "isometric." Under each strengthening exercise is a section, *Muscular Work*. This tells you the location of the muscle or muscles you are using in that exercise. The section, *Anatomy*, at the start of each region will also help you to understand the location and action of the muscles in each region.

6. Isometric exercises are helpful in two ways. First, in developing the muscle's ability to exert force at that muscle length; and second, to let you localize and concentrate on the sensation of where the muscular tension is coming from. Your awareness of muscular tensions can be helpful in teaching you more about your body.

For example, if you become aware of the sensation of tension in the hip abductor region when you are *not* exercising, you will be able to recognize this. You will know to spend extra time on hip abductor *stretches* for a few days to reduce the muscular tension and elongate the shortened muscle fibers. And when you know what leg movement produces abduction, you can analyze your recent activities and see what it is you've been doing that overstressed that muscle region.

You can use this method after skiing to analyze your skiing positions. (It may take about a day for your muscular soreness to develop.) You can get an idea of body movements you have been stressing more than others and movements that may be over-compensations for the underuse of other, more efficient positions.

7. For the average, recreational skier, performing strengthening exercises with the weight of your body parts alone and doing up to 15 repetitions will be sufficient. However, some exercises are better done with weights, for it would take too many repetitions for the muscle to work hard enough to become stronger. These exercises are written with instructions for adding weights under *Progressions* after the exercise.

Specific Instructions for Weights

When you use weights for added resistance you should determine the maximal weight that you can use and still do 10 repetitions. These are complete repetitions, in good form. You should find the last few repetitions of the 10 difficult, but not impossible to complete properly.

Increase the amount of weight in one-pound increments. If your movements are jerky and strained, then the weight you are using is too heavy for you.

Do a total of 3 sets (10 repetitions in each) for each weight exercise.

The first set uses one-half of the maximum weight for a warm-up.

The second set uses the full maximum weight for the work-out.

The third set uses less than half of the maximum weight for a speed workout. (For skiing you want to move with strength and with quickness.)

9 | The Physical Fitness Quiz

You will need a well-padded floor, exercise mat, or padded table, a couple of large pillows, a tape measure, and a stopwatch or a watch with a sweep hand. You should allow at least half an hour. Don't start this quiz unless you have time to do it in a relaxed manner. Wear comfortable clothing, the same as you would wear for exercising. It's more convenient and more fun if two or more people work together. While one person takes the quiz, the other assists in the measuring and records the results.

Record all of the results on the Physical Fitness Quiz Recording Sheet at the end of this chapter. In the "failed by" column, write in the amount by which you missed the standard.

FITNESS QUIZ   PART ONE

Test 1   Double Leg Lift Supine

Starting position: Lie on your back with both legs straight on the floor.

Instructions: Raise both legs only 10 inches from the floor. Keep your knees completely straight. Hold this position for 10 seconds.

Recording: Grade yourself "pass" only if you can easily maintain both legs in the air for 10 seconds.

Remedial Exercises: Strengthen Abdominals, Chapter 14. Strengthen Hip Flexors, Chapter 16.

IMPORTANT NOTE: This Double Leg Lift is *not* an exercise and should not be attempted as an exercise. It is for testing purposes only! If you see that you cannot perform it easily, STOP TRYING and grade yourself "fail."

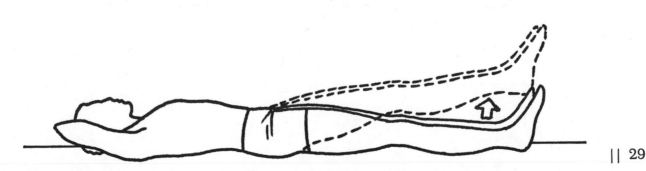

Test 1

Test 2   Straight Knee Sit-Up

Starting position: Have someone hold your feet down. If you have no assistance, hook your feet under a heavy piece of furniture. Keep your hands behind your head.

Instructions: Do *not* bend your knees! Raise up to a full sitting position.

Recording: Grade yourself "pass" only if you complete the full sit-up easily. Otherwise grade yourself by percentage. 50 percent for coming up halfway, 25 percent for coming up one-fourth of the way, etc.

Remedial Exercises: Strengthen Abdominals, Chapter 14. Strengthen Hip Flexors, Chapter 16.

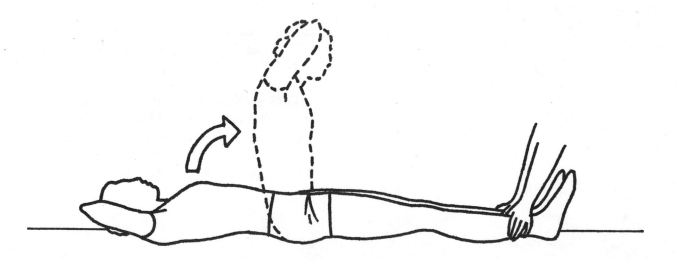

Test 2

Test 3 Bent Knee Sit Up

Starting position: Have someone hold your feet down with your knees bent, feet flat on the floor and close to buttocks. If you have no assistance hook your feet under a piece of furniture. Keep your hands clasped behind your head.

Instructions: Raise up to a full sitting position.

Recording: Grade yourself "pass" only if you can complete the full sit-up easily. Otherwise grade yourself by percentage. 50 percent for coming up halfway, 25 percent for coming up one-fourth of the way, etc.

Remedial Exercises: Strengthen Abdominals, Chapter 14.

Test 3

Test 4 Upper Trunk Lift

Starting position: Lie face down over a large pillow with hands clasped behind your head and hips and legs held down by another person. If you have no assistance, slip your feet under a heavy piece of furniture.

Instructions: Raise upper trunk until horizontal. Hold this position for 10 seconds.

Recording: Grade yourself "pass" only if you can easily maintain the trunk lift for 10 seconds.

Remedial Exercises: Strengthen Upper Back Extensors, Chapter 15.

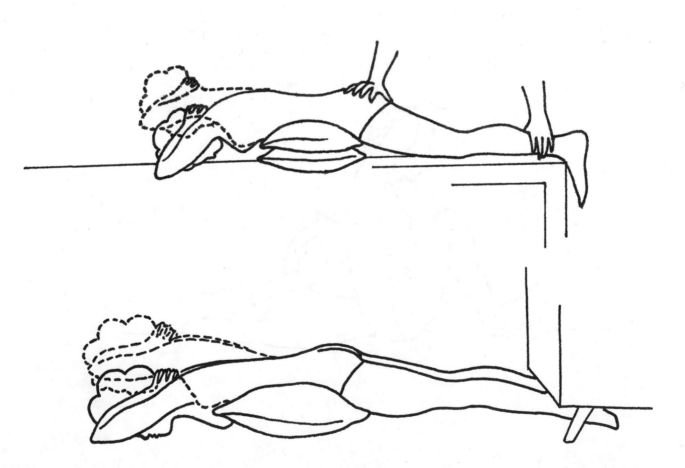

Test 4

Test 5 Double Leg Lift Prone

Starting position: Lie face down over a large pillow with another person holding your upper trunk down. If you have no assistance, hold onto the bottom of a sturdy piece of furniture to stabilize the upper body.

Instructions: Raise both legs in the air and hold them in position for 10 seconds.

Recording: Grade yourself "pass" only if you can easily maintain both legs lifted for 10 seconds.

Remedial Exercises: Strengthen Lower Back Extensors, Chapter 15. Strengthen Hip Extensors, Chapter 21.

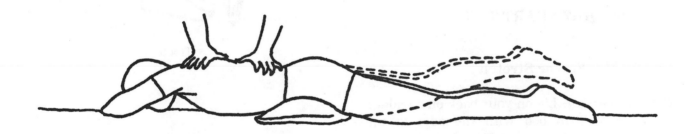

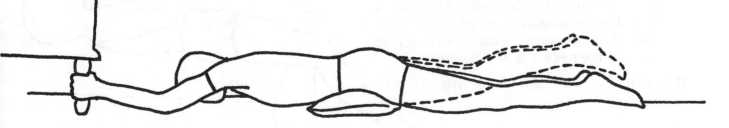

Test 5

Test 6   Fingertips to Floor

Starting position: Stand with your feet shoulder
    width apart. Keep your knees straight.
Instructions: Bend over by curling down to
    touch your fingertips to the floor.
Recording: Grade yourself "pass" only if finger-
    tips (or more of hand) touch the floor.
    Otherwise grade yourself by the distance in
    inches from your fingertips to the floor.
Remedial Exercises: Limbering Routine for relax-
    ation, Chapter 11. Stretching Back Exten-
    sors, Chapter 15. Stretching Hamstrings,
    Chapter 17.

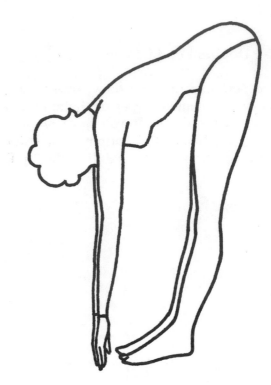

Test 6

FITNESS QUIZ   PART TWO

Test 7   Hip Flexor Stretch

Starting position: Lie on your back on a padded
    table or firm bed with the edge at the
    middle of your thighs. Bend both knees up
    to your chest.

Instructions: Hold one knee bent up to your
    chest while you let the other leg dangle
    over the edge of the table.

Recording: Grade yourself "pass" if the dan-
    gling leg can touch the table edge without
    your having to move the knee that is at
    your chest. Measure the distance from your
    thigh to the table if it does not touch.

Remedial Exercise: Stretching Hip Flexors,
    Chapter 16.

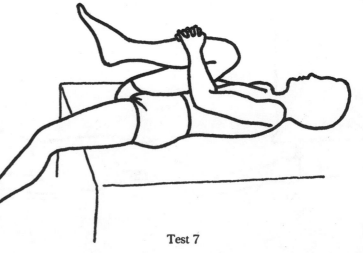

Test 7

Test 8   Straight Leg Raising

Starting position: Lie on your back with both legs straight.

Instructions: Keep one leg fully straightened, lift it as far as you can toward the ceiling without bending your knee.

Recording: Grade yourself "pass" if your leg reaches an angle of 80 to 90 degrees (90 is the full vertical position). Estimate the angle your leg makes from the horizontal.

Remedial Exercises: Stretching Hamstrings, Chapter 17.

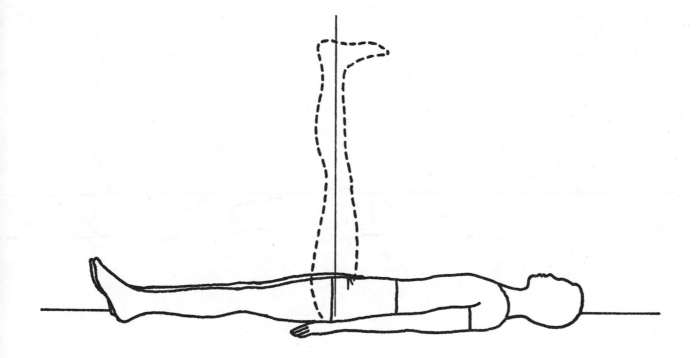

Test 8

Test 9   Ankle Bending

Starting position: Lie on your back with both legs straight.

Instructions: Point your feet toward your head.

Recording: Grade yourself "pass" if your feet come up to at least 90 degrees (vertical). Estimate angle lacking from vertical.

Remedial Exercises: Stretching of Calf, Chapter 22.

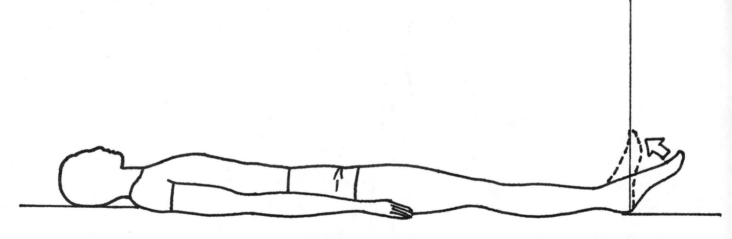

Test 9

Test 10   Leg Spread

Starting position: Sit on the floor in the full upright position with both legs spread apart.

Instructions: Keep knees straight and spread legs to at least a 90-degree angle. Straddle the corner of a rug to judge the angle.

Recording: Grade yourself "pass" if you reach at least 90 degrees. Estimate angle if you do not reach 90 degrees.

Remedial Exercises: Stretching Hip Adductors, Chapter 18.

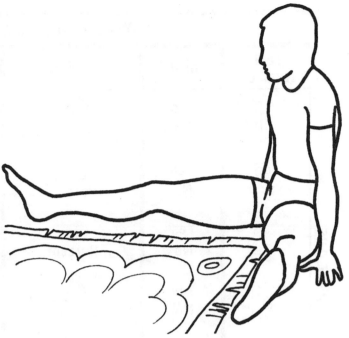

Test 10

Test 11   Wall Sitting

Starting position: Lean your back against a wall with your feet 12 to 18 inches away from the wall.

Instructions: Slide down the wall as if sitting on an imaginary chair. Check that your thighs are parallel with the floor. Adjust your feet until they are directly beneath your knees.

Recording: Grade yourself "pass" if you can hold the "sitting" position for 1 minute.

Remedial Exercises: Strengthen Knee Extensors, Chapter 16.

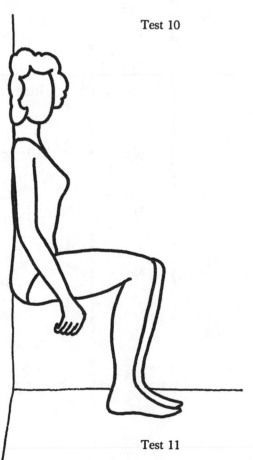

Test 11

PHYSICAL FITNESS QUIZ RECORDING SHEET

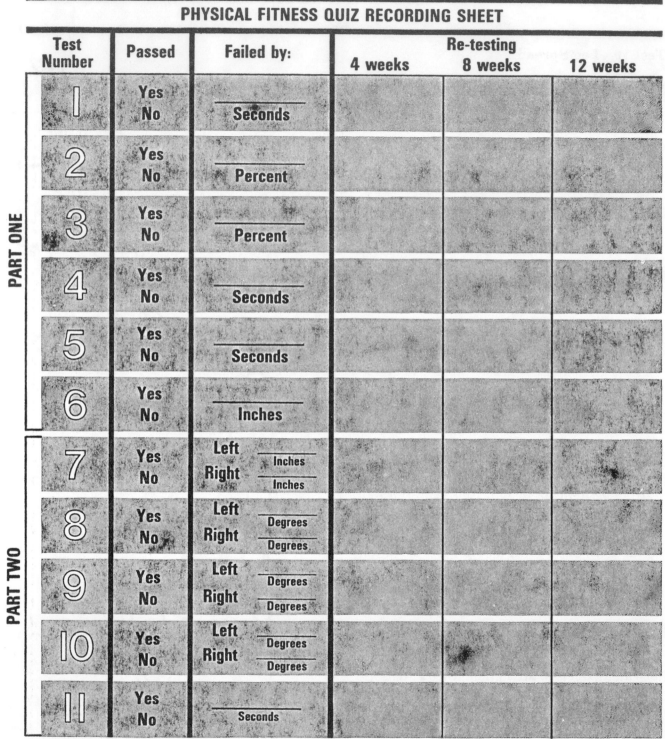

	Test Number	Passed	Failed by:	Re-testing 4 weeks	8 weeks	12 weeks
PART ONE	1	Yes No	_____ Seconds			
	2	Yes No	_____ Percent			
	3	Yes No	_____ Percent			
	4	Yes No	_____ Seconds			
	5	Yes No	_____ Seconds			
	6	Yes No	_____ Inches			
PART TWO	7	Yes No	Left _____ Inches / Right _____ Inches			
	8	Yes No	Left _____ Degrees / Right _____ Degrees			
	9	Yes No	Left _____ Degrees / Right _____ Degrees			
	10	Yes No	Left _____ Degrees / Right _____ Degrees			
	11	Yes No	_____ Seconds			

10 || Basic Program Planning Chart

	Initial	Repetitions / Weight	4 Weeks	Repetitions / Weight	8 Weeks	Repetitions / Weight
I—NECK						
Stretching						
1 Five-way head stretch						
Strengthening						
2 Neck resistance, isometric						
3 Shrugging						
II—SHOULDER, etc.						
Stretching						
4 Shoulder blade squeeze						
5 Shoulder hugging						
6 Elbow spread						
7 Rotation stretch						
8 Triceps stretch						
9 Double underarm stretch						
10 Hands and knees upper body stretch						
Strengthening						
11 Chair dip						
12 Wall push-up						
13 Chair push-up						
14 Standard push-up, knees bent						
15 Bench push-up						
16 Standard push-up, knees extended						
III—TRUNK, FLEXION						
Stretching						
17 Full body stretch, backlying						
18 Cobra stretch						
19 Standing side bend						
20 Sitting trunk rotation						
21 Standing trunk rotation						

	Initial	Repetitions / Weight	4 Weeks	Repetitions / Weight	8 Weeks	Repetitions / Weight
Strengthening						
22 Head Raise (a)						
Head Raise (b)						
23 Partial sit-up						
24 Full sit-up						
25 Rotated sit-ups						
26 Knee-kiss						
27 Pelvic tilt						
28 Cat back						
29 Double knee roll						
30 Alternate elbow touch						
31 Ankle grasp						
32 Side trunk raise						

IV—TRUNK, EXTENSION

	Initial	Repetitions / Weight	4 Weeks	Repetitions / Weight	8 Weeks	Repetitions / Weight
Stretching						
33 Sitting bend						
34 Rotated sitting bend						
35 Total body roll						
36 Counter-rotated body twist						
37 Backward roll over						
38 Standing floor touch						
Strengthening						
39 Alternate arm and/or leg lift						
40 Upper back lift						
41 Double leg lift						

V—FRONT OF THIGH AND HIP JOINT

	Initial	Repetitions / Weight	4 Weeks	Repetitions / Weight	8 Weeks	Repetitions / Weight
Stretching						
42 Backlying hip flexor stretch						
43 Standing hip flexor stretch						
44 Double front thigh stretch						
45 Sidelying thigh stretch						
46 Standing front thigh stretch						
Strengthening						
47 Rotated leg raise						
48 Hip flexor strengthener						
49 Quadriceps setting, isometric						
50 Wall sitting, isometric						
51 Knee extension, sitting						

	Initial	Repetitions / Weight	4 Weeks	Repetitions / Weight	8 Weeks	Repetitions / Weight
VI—BACK OF THIGH						
Stretching						
52 Aerial hamstring stretch						
53 Single leg hamstring stretch						
54 Special remedial hamstring stretch						
55 V-spread hamstring stretch						
56 Double leg hamstring stretch						
57 Standing hamstring stretch						
Strengthening						
58 Prone knee flexion						
59 Standing knee flexion						
60 Sitting knee flexion, isometric						
61 Prone knee flexion, isometric						
62 Self-resisted knee flexion						
VII—INNER THIGH						
Stretching						
63 Adductor spread, sitting						
64 Adductor spread, knees bent						
65 Adductor stretch, standing						
66 Adductor stretch, backlying						
67 Combination stretch						
Strengthening						
68 Horizontal leg swing						
69 Sidelying lower leg lift						
70 Chair squeeze, isometric						
71 Partner squeeze, isometric						
72 Sitting thigh squeeze						
VIII—OUTER THIGH AND OUTER HIP						
Stretching						
73 Sidelying hip stretch						
36 Counter-rotated body twist						
Strengthening						
74 Sidelying upper leg lift						
75 Side leg lift, standing						
76 Chair spread, isometric						
77 Partner thigh squeeze, isometric						

	Initial	Repetitions / Weight	4 Weeks	Repetitions / Weight	8 Weeks	Repetitions / Weight
IX—HIP ROTATIONS						
Stretching: Internal Rotation						
36 Counter-rotated body twist						
78 Hip rotation, prone						
79 Leg cross over						
Stretching: External Rotation						
64 Adductor spread, knees bent						
78 Hip rotation, prone						
79 Leg cross over						
Strengthening						
78 Hip rotation, prone						
79 Leg cross over						
80 Self-resisted rotation, external						
81 Self-resisted rotation, internal						
X—HIP EXTENSION						
Stretching						
35 Total body roll						
37 Backward roll over						
52 Aerial hamstring stretch						
Strengthening						
82 Buttock squeeze						
83 Buttock lift						
84 Single leg lift, prone						
85 Bent knee leg raise, prone						
86 Rear leg lift, standing						
87 Scissors kicking						
XI—CALF AND ANKLE						
Stretching						
88 Calf stretch, toward a wall						
89 Calf stretch, standing						
Strengthening						
90 Toe stands						
91 Partner foot push						

11 || Warm-Up for the Basic Program

LIMBERING EXERCISES: FLOOR ROUTINE

A series of limbering movements consists of 3 to 5 repetitions of each exercise. These are very easy, floating movements that should take very little effort and very little power. You can start directly on the floor or stand up first and do a few Standing Side Bends (exercise 19) before the rest of the limbering routine.

Start on your back with both knees bent, feet flat on the floor. Use a small pillow under your head, or no pillow at all. Do the exercises in the order given below.

1. Breathe deeply in through your nose, and exhale fully by blowing air out of your mouth. Repeat only two or three times.

2. Pick up your head and look at your knees. Keep your chin tucked down toward your chest. Lower your head to the floor, then lazily roll it from side to side, letting it drop as if very heavy at the far right and far left sides.

3. Shrug your shoulders. Slide them up and keep them up toward your ears for a moment, then let them lower slowly and relax completely before repeating.

Starting position for Limbering Exercises 1 through 3

4. Raise one of your bent knees toward your chest. Place the foot back on the floor again, and let your leg go limp and heavy. Let it straighten out fully on the floor. Wobble your leg a few times to release more tension from it, then slide it back up to the starting position. Repeat, alternating legs.

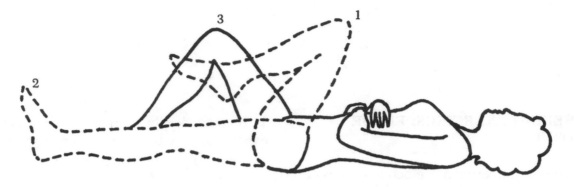

Limbering Exercise 4

5. Turn to lie on your side with both knees bent. Place a small pillow under your head for comfort and relaxation of your neck. Raise the uppermost knee toward your chest, and without stopping move it from there to a straight position behind you. Finally return it to the starting position. Rest the leg completely before repeating the sequence. Turn and repeat on the other side.

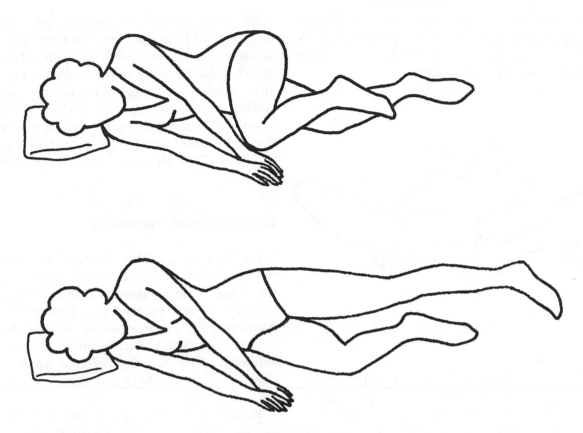

Limbering Exercise 5

6. Turn to lie on your back again. Raise both arms in the air with your hands pointing up toward the ceiling. Alternately stretch each arm higher as if trying to touch the ceiling.

7. Still on your back, make large circles in the air with both arms clockwise and counterclockwise.

8. Turn onto your stomach. Place a large pillow underneath your abdomen so that your spine is rounded over the pillow. Squeeze your buttocks together for a few seconds. Then release the tension to relax the muscles completely before repeating.

9. Lie on your back again. Bend both knees and place your feet on the floor. Keep your knees touching together, and gently roll them from side to side. Keep your shoulders in contact with the floor at all times.

10. On your back, keep your knees bent, place your feet together, and spread your knees apart. Easily and gently move your knees together, then apart, together and apart. This is done to "jiggle" your thighs, not to try to spread your thighs as far apart as you can.

Limbering Exercise 10

The limbering routine is used at the beginning of an exercise session for a warm-up and at the conclusion of a session for cooling off. As a warm-up, do the exercises in order from 1 to 10. As a cool-off, reverse the order and do them from 10 to 1.

Breathing Exercises can be done at any time during an exercise session. Use them to relax and release body tension.

Diaphragmatic Breathing

Lie in a comfortable position on your back with a small pillow under your head. Place your hands lightly on your abdomen, just above your navel. Inhale slowly and deeply through your nose, filling your lungs so that the air coming in pushes your hands upward. Exhale slowly and completely through your mouth, blowing the air through pursed lips. Make the exhale complete by blowing out all the air that you possibly can.

Lateral-Costal Breathing

Lie in a comfortable position on your back with a small pillow under your head. Place one hand lightly on each side of your rib cage. Inhale slowly and deeply through your nose, expanding your ribcage width as you do. The inspired air should force your hands to move sideward. Exhale fully through your mouth, blowing air until there is nothing left to blow out.

In both types of breathing, be certain that you are not shrugging your shoulders and heaving your upper chest up and down as a substitute for the proper, localized inspirations and expirations. Practice in front of a mirror if you want to see if you are using a lot of accessory and unnecessary motions.

INTERMITTENT RELAXATION EXERCISES

These are exercises that are part of the Basic Program but are also useful as general relaxation positions. At any time during your exercise session, use the following exercises before going on to another exercise in your program. These positions are stretching positions that stretch many parts of the body at the same time.

• Hands and Knees Upper Body Stretch (Region II), exercise 10

• Full Body Stretch, Backlying (Region III), exercise 17

• Total Body Roll (Region IV), exercise 35

• Backward Roll Over (Region IV), exercise 37

In addition, there's another relaxation position that is particularly comfortable after doing adductor or hamstring stretching exercises. It's called the Leg Bounce. Sit on the floor with both legs straight out in front of you. Place your hands on the floor behind you. Keeping your buttocks and heels on the floor, lightly bounce the back of your thighs and calves on the floor to help release tension throughout the entire leg. Bounce both legs at the same time or do each individually. Bounce about 25 times.

12 | Region I—The Neck (Movements of the Head)

ANATOMY

The muscles at the back of the neck attach to the upper vertebrae of the spinal column, the base of the skull and the top of the shoulder blades. Contraction of these muscles tilts the head backward, to the side, and shrugs the shoulders toward the ears.

Exercises for the front of the neck are found in this region as well as in the abdominal strengthening region. These neck muscles attach to the collarbone and the base of the skull. On contraction they move the head downward and rotate it from side to side.

FUNCTION

Good strength of all of these muscles is important for protecting the neck structures in falls.

Good flexibility lets you turn your head freely and fully. It's important to look ahead to where you're going, to keep your head relaxed when skiing, especially over bumpy terrain, and to be able to turn your head quickly to see skiers in the periphery of your vision.

It is very important to recognize neck tension when it is starting, and to start stretching and relaxation exercises right away to reduce the stiffness and discomfort of excessive muscular tightening. A tight neck will affect the function of your shoulder blades and shoulders. Restricted, tight head movements make it harder for all of your body's normal balancing mechanisms to work smoothly.

CATEGORY: STRETCHING

1. Five-Way Head Stretch

Starting position: Sit in a comfortable chair in an upright position.

Action: Tilt your head upward and look at the ceiling. Be sure that you are moving your head and not just your eyes. Hold the stretch for 10 seconds.

The stretch: Front of the neck and under the chin.

Action: Let your head drop downward toward your chest, chin tucked down. Hold the stretch for 10 seconds.

The stretch: Back of the head and neck and between the shoulder blades.

Variation: Keep your head down and roll it slightly to each side.

Extension   Flexion

Action: Tilt your head to the side, but keep facing forward. Let your ear drop as close as possible toward your shoulder. Keep your head limp and relaxed. Hold thé stretch 10 seconds to each side.

The stretch: On the side of the neck, opposite to the direction of the tilt.

Action: Keep your head erect as in the starting position and turn to look over one shoulder. Be careful that your chin does not drop down to your shoulder. Be sure that your shoulder does not rise up toward your chin. Hold the stretch for 10 seconds to each side.

The stretch: On the side of the neck opposite to the direction of the turn.

Action: Neck Straightener (not illustrated)

Starting position: Begin with your head in its normal forward position. Tuck your chin inward at the same time that you try to make your neck as tall as possible. Hold this stretch for 10 seconds. Repeat.

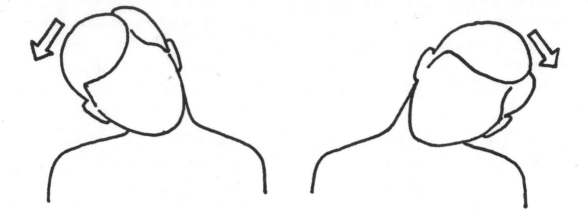

Side Bending

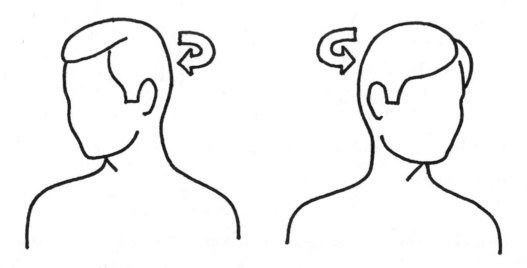

Rotation

CATEGORY: STRENGTHENING

2. Neck Resistance, Isometric

Starting position: Place your palm on your forehead.

Action: Try to move your head forward, but resist the movement with your palm so that there is no motion. Hold for 5 seconds. Relax and repeat.

Muscular work: Front of the neck.

Variation: Place your palm on the side of your head to resist the movements of side tilting and rotation. Alternately resist right and left sides.

Progression: Combine the isometric holding motions with the stretching positions for each direction.

Resist forward movement for 5 seconds, then let your head drop forward for 10 seconds.

Resist backward movement for 5 seconds, then lift and stretch your head back for 10 seconds.

Resist turning to each side for 5 seconds, then follow each holding motion with the stretch position for 10 seconds.

Resist tilting to each side for 5 seconds and follow immediately by tilting to that side for 10 seconds.

Lie on your back and press your head backward into a firm pillow or a padded floor for 5 seconds.

Change the forward flexion isometric into a "moving" exercise by pressing your palm against your forehead but allowing your head to move downward very slowly. Give resistance from your hand throughout the entire excursion of your head.

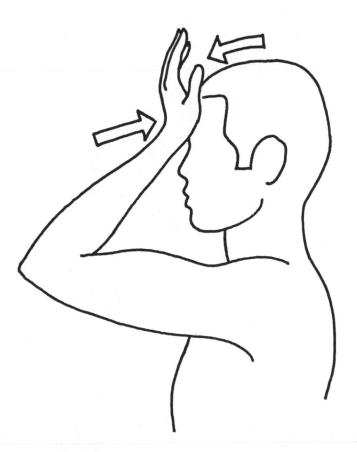

3. Shrugging (not illustrated)

Starting position: Sit or stand with your shoulders in their normal posture.

Action: Shrug both shoulders up toward your ears. Hold this position for 5 seconds. This is the direction of shoulder elevation (see illustration). Lower to the starting position by letting them drop downward. Relax shoulder muscles completely before repeating.

Muscular work: Between the shoulders and the neck.

Progression: Hold weights in each hand and perform the shrugging motion as in the standard exercise.

Comments: This exercise is included in the neck region because the muscles that produce it extend along the neck to the back of the head.

In the standard exercise, the relaxation phase with the shoulders dropped down to their normal position is very important. This exercise is helpful for the release of muscular tension in the back of the neck if it is done throughout the day.

13 | Region II—Shoulder, Shoulder Girdle, Upper Chest and Upper Arm

ANATOMY

The muscles of the shoulder, shoulder girdle, and upper chest attach to the bones of the shoulder blade (scapula), collarbone (clavicle), ribs, and upper arm (humerus). The muscles controlling the elbow joint attach from the front of the shoulder and humerus to the front of the elbow for flexion (biceps and other muscles); and from the back of the shoulder and humerus to the rear of the elbow for extension (triceps).

Of the many movements produced by contraction of these muscles, the most significant for downhill skiers are backward and downward movements of the arms and shoulder blades. Primarily, these are the movement directions of shoulder blade depression and adduction, shoulder extension and elbow extension. Cross-country skiers in particular require a good range of mobility in the direction of shoulder flexion.

The other movements of rotation, shoulder abduction and adduction, while not stressed excessively by skiers, do play an important role in shoulder function. In cases of shoulder injury, it is imperative that normal strength and mobility be restored in all of these different planes of motion. If you are doing rehabilitative exercises from Chapter 34, refer to the illustrations shown here to remind yourself of all of the possible movements for this region of the body.

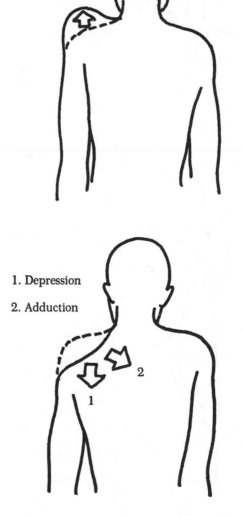

Shoulder Girdle

Elevation

1. Depression
2. Adduction

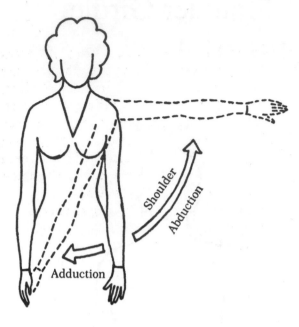

Shoulder Abduction

Adduction

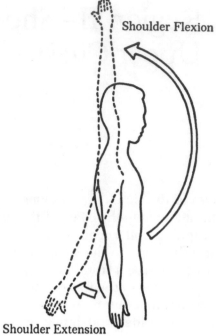

Shoulder Flexion

Shoulder Extension

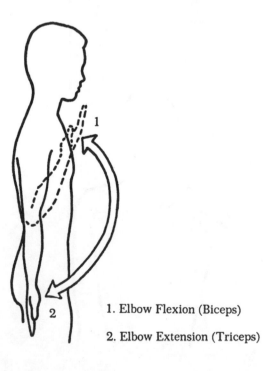

1. Elbow Flexion (Biceps)

2. Elbow Extension (Triceps)

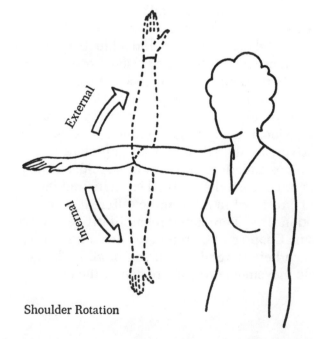

External

Internal

Shoulder Rotation

FUNCTION

Skiers use their shoulders, upper arms and chest muscles to exert force on their poles. This occurs when double or alternately poling on level ground, climbing uphill and getting up from falls. In addition, quick bursts of action with the arms are needed for some types of turns where the body's movements are explosive and involve sudden changes in direction, as in aggressive, mogul skiing. Here, good strength and mobility of all segments of the arms gives the skier the symmetry and balance needed for planting his poles with stability.

CATEGORY: STRETCHING

Special Instructions

The shoulder region has seven different stretching exercises. Some of them stretch the same muscles but from different positions, while others stretch entirely different muscles. In the shoulder region you must do more than one stretching exercise to be sure that you are stretching all of the muscles and not just some of them. This will bring the shoulder region through all of its planes of movement.

You must include the following exercises:

Exercise 4 plus 5 or substitute 6 by itself
Exercise 7
Exercise 8
Exercise 9 or 10

4. Shoulder Blade Squeeze

Starting position: Stand with both hands clasped behind your back.

Action: Raise both hands off of your back, keeping elbows straight. As the hands are raised, squeeze both shoulder blades together. Hold stretch for 10 seconds. Relax and repeat.

The stretch: Above the inner elbow, across the front of the upper chest and shoulders.

Variation: Hold a towel, umbrella, or broomstick behind your back with your hands shoulder width apart. Raise hands as instructed above.

Comments: This movement can be done throughout the day to help ease shoulder tension.

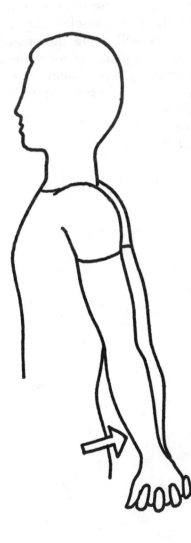

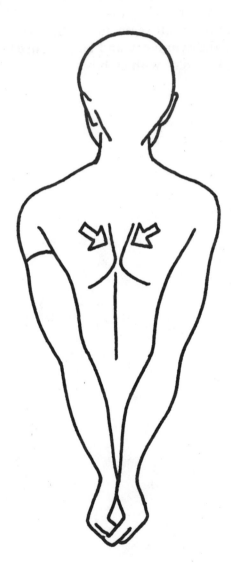

5. Shoulder Hugging (not illustrated)

Starting position: Stand or sit with each hand wrapped around the opposite shoulder.

Action: Use a gently pulling motion with your hands to try to spread your shoulder blades apart. Lower your chin toward your chest to increase the pull between the shoulder blades.

The stretch: Across the neck, upper back, and between the shoulder blades.

Comments: This movement can be done throughout the day to help ease shoulder and neck tension.

6. Elbow Spread

Starting position: Lie on your back with both hands clasped behind your neck.

Action: Spread your elbows apart as far as possible. Hold position for 15 seconds. Relax and repeat.

The stretch: In the armpits and upper chest.

Action: Bring elbows as close together as you can. Hold position for 15 seconds. Relax and repeat.

The stretch: Between the shoulder blades.

Variations: These movements can both be done sitting, standing, or lying down.

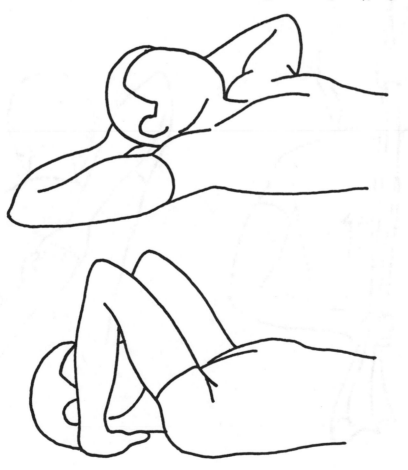

7. Rotation Stretch

Starting position: Stand holding a towel behind you, with one hand at your lower back and the other hand behind your neck.

Action: Holding firmly onto the towel with both hands, use the uppermost hand to raise the lower one toward the center of your back. Pull until your lower hand cannot go any higher up your back. Reverse hand positions to stretch the other arm. Hold the stretch for 10 seconds.

The stretch: In the front of the shoulder of the lower arm.

Variation: Do not use a towel. Place the upper hand and the lower hand in the middle of your back, and hook the fingers of both hands together. This adds a stretch to the underside of the upper arm, above the armpit.

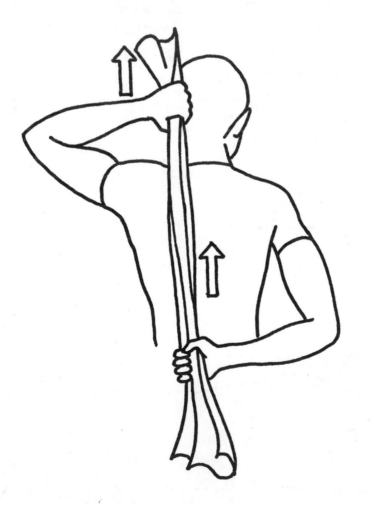

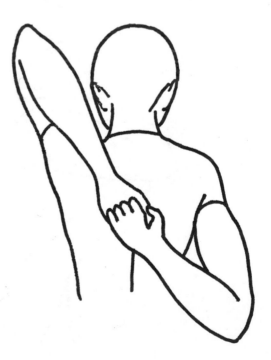

8. Triceps Stretch

Starting position: Stand with one arm overhead, the elbow bent and the hand resting in the center of your neck. Place your other hand on top of the bent elbow.

Action: Use your hand to pull your elbow closer to your head. This causes your hand to reach down your spine. Hold this pull for 10 seconds. Relax and repeat. Reverse arm positions to stretch the other arm.

The stretch: Along the underside of the raised, bent arm and below the armpit.

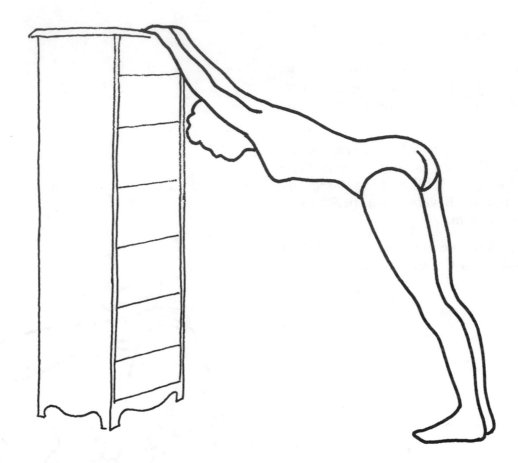

9. Double Underarm Stretch

Starting position: Stand with both hands on top of a tall dresser or refrigerator. Step back with both feet until you feel a mild stretch under your arms. Feet should remain flat on the floor.

Action: Lower your head between your arms and let your upper body hang from your hands. Hold the stretch for 10 seconds. Relax and repeat.

The stretch: Underneath both shoulders and along the sides of the upper trunk.

Variation: To increase the stretch to lower parts of the side of the trunk, keep your hands and feet in the same position but slowly shift your hips to one side.

Comments: This is good for the shoulder and upper trunk flexibility needed by cross-country skiers.

10. Hands and Knees Upper Body Stretch

Starting position: On the floor, assume a hands and knees position with the knees directly below your hips.

Action: Keep your legs in place, but slide your hands forward with your head between your arms. If your hips begin to move forward too, then you have gone too far. Hold the stretch for 30 seconds. Relax and repeat.

The stretch: Along the underside of the upper arms and the outer sides of the shoulder blades.

Comments: If you also feel a stretch along the *top* of your shoulders, be sure to include the Rotation Stretch exercise in your Basic Program.

The following Region II strengthening exercises include several versions of the basic "push-up" exercise. Start with the variation that is most comfortable for you, but be sure to include some type of "push-up" in your Basic Program. If you have a particular problem with stiffness or loss of mobility of the shoulders, refer to the chapter on rehabilitation for additional shoulder flexibility exercises.

To balance the muscular work that you achieve in push-up exercises, it's a good idea to do "pull-up" or "chinning" exercises. Many people are strong enough to handle their own body weight and do a standard pull-up from a suspended position, dangling beneath the bar.

Many more people are unable to perform this exercise. Instead, they can develop strength by doing "negative pull-ups." To do this stand on a stool underneath a chinning bar, your hands gripping the bar, and your palms facing you. Standing on the stool you should be high enough and close enough to the bar so that your chin is at the level or just below the level of the bar. Next, lift your feet off of the stool so that you are hanging with your chin at the level of the bar. (If you are below it, you will have to jump up slightly to start with your chin at bar level.) Then very slowly lower yourself by letting your arms gradually extend until you reach the full dangling position. Keep your knees bent so that your feet don't hit the stool on the way down. Repeat.

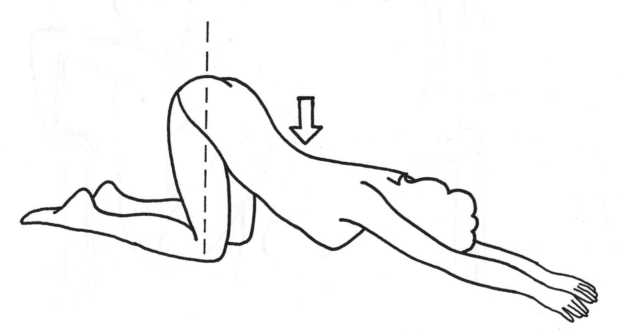

CATEGORY: STRENGTHENING

11. Chair Dip

Starting position: Sit on the edge of a sturdy chair, low table or bed with your knees bent and feet flat on the floor.

Action: Slowly lower yourself toward the floor supporting yourself by your hands on the chair seat sides. Do not sit down on the floor. Use your arms to push you back up to the starting position.

Muscular work: Upper arms above the elbow and below the shoulder blades.

Comments: This exercise gives a good stretch to the front of the shoulder when you are in the lowered position.

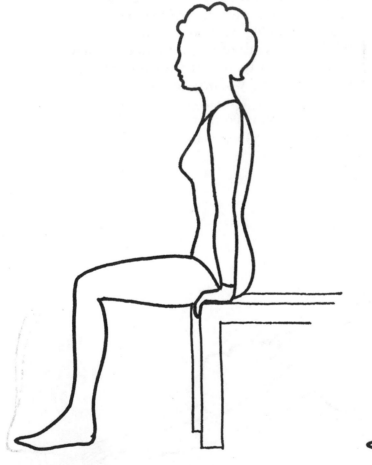
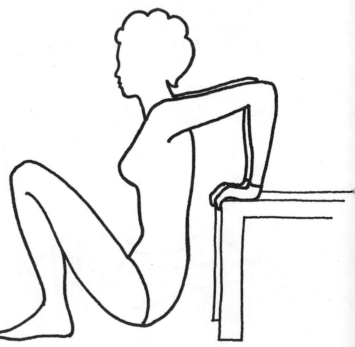

12. Wall Push-Up

Starting position: Stand facing a wall, arms' length away. Place both hands on the wall at shoulder height. Step back so that your body is straight, but you are leaning on a slight angle toward the wall.

Action: Slowly, lower your forehead to the wall by bending your elbows, keeping your back straight. Make sure that you do not merely bob your head toward the wall. Then slowly straighten your arms to push you back to the starting position. Keep your palms in contact with the wall at all times; do not move your feet. Repeat.

Muscular work: In the upper arms above your elbows.

Variation: Spread your hands farther apart on the wall, but still at shoulder height. This position uses musculature in the front of the upper chest.

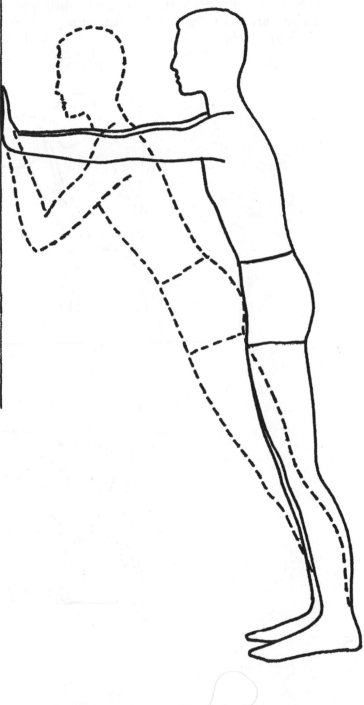

13. Chair Push-Up

Starting position: Stand facing a sturdy chair. Place both hands shoulder width apart on the side edges of the seat. Step back until your elbows are fully extended. Lean with pressure on your hands.

Action: Slowly lower your forehead to the chair seat by bending your elbows. Slowly straighten your elbows to return to the starting position. Repeat.

Muscular work: In the upper arms above your elbows.

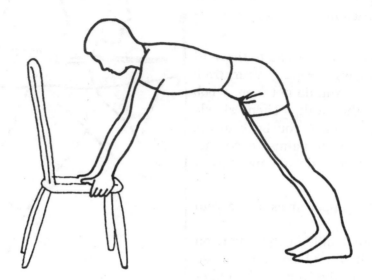

14. Standard Push-Up, Knees Bent (More difficult) (not illustrated)

Starting position: On the floor, assume a hands and knees position with hands directly underneath the shoulders.

Action: Keep your knees in place, and slowly lower your forehead to the floor by bending your elbows. Slowly straighten your elbows to return to the starting position. Repeat.

Muscular work: In the upper arms above the elbows.

Variation: Spread the hands more than shoulder width apart to use musculature in the front of the upper chest. Use the open hand position, or if you have wrist discomfort this way, keep your hand closed and your wrist straight.

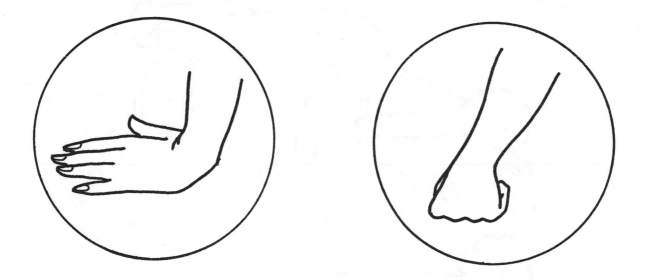

15. Bench Push-Up

Starting position: Lie on your stomach supported by a low, padded bench or the edge of your bed. Place your hands on the floor directly underneath your shoulders.

Action: Slowly lower your forehead to the floor by bending your elbows. Slowly straighten your elbows to return to the starting position. Repeat.

Muscular work: In the upper arms above the elbows.

Variation: Spread hands farther than shoulder width apart to use musculature in the front of the upper chest.

Comments: This version of the push-up is particularly good for people who find chair push-ups too easy and standard push-ups too difficult. It is recommended for people who have knee problems who should not use the hands and knees position.

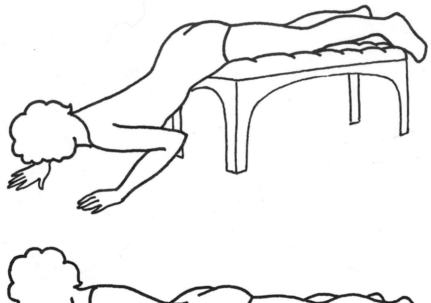

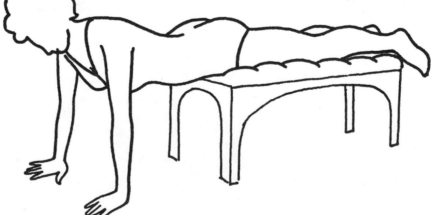

16. Standard Push-Up, Knees Extended (Most difficult)

Starting position: Lie on your stomach on the floor with your hands directly beneath your shoulders.

Action: Push yourself up from the floor by straightening your elbows completely. When your elbows are fully extended, only your toes and hands should be contacting the floor. Your knees should be straight and your body horizontal. Return to the floor by slowly bending your elbows. Repeat.

Muscular work: In the upper arms above the elbows.

Variation: Spread your hands farther apart than shoulder width to use musculature in the upper part of the chest.

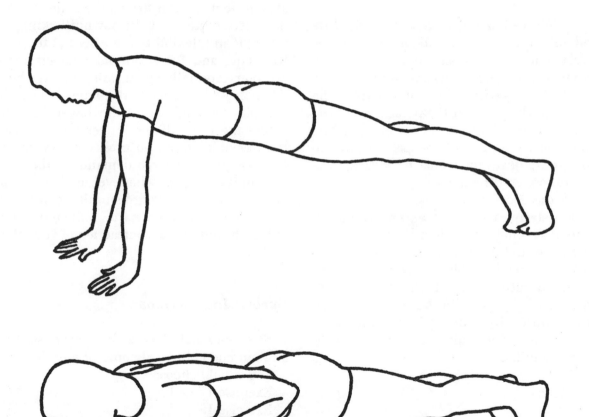

14 || Region III—Trunk (Flexion)

ANATOMY

The muscles of trunk flexion are primarily the abdominal muscles. The abdominal muscles consist of some muscle fibers running vertically and others running obliquely across the front of the trunk. The vertical fibers attach from the lower edge of the pelvis at the pubic bone to the lower ribs. The oblique fibers attach from the ribs and the front rims of the pelvis. The abdominal group flexes the trunk in forward, sideward, and rotated directions.

Due to the location of these muscle fibers, abdominal strength plays an extremely important role in keeping stress off of the lower spine. Contraction of the abdominals rolls the pelvis in a backward direction. This takes some of the excessive curvature out of the lower spine which is usually present in the type of chronic backache caused by faulty posture and weak muscles. Weak abdominals and weak backs usually go hand in hand.

FUNCTION

Flexibility of the trunk allows you to rotate your upper body easily. Vigorous cross-country arm movements can stretch the oblique abdominal fibers quite a bit. In downhill skiing, both strength and flexibility are essential for general balancing and for continual changes in body position, especially when skiing in large bumps. "Anticipated" turns that require upper body turning downhill while the lower body faces across the hill call for limber trunk musculature. Double poling on cross-country or downhill skis places a large demand on the abdominal muscle group whenever both arms push downward and backward simultaneously. (Push both your hands down hard on the top of a table to feel the automatic contraction of your abdominal muscles.)

Special Instructions

Be sure to include stretching exercises for the straight and oblique abdominal muscles.
You should choose:
Exercise 17 or 18
Exercise 19
Exercise 20 or 21

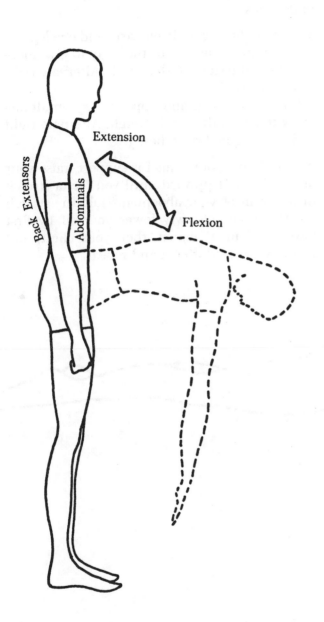

Extension

Back Extensors

Abdominals

Flexion

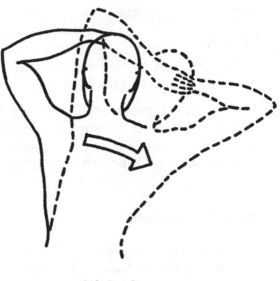

Side Bending

Rotation

CATEGORY: STRETCHING

17. Full Body Stretch, Backlying (not illustrated)

Starting position: Lie flat on your back with both arms stretched overhead on the floor and both legs straight on the floor.

Action: Stretch your arms to make them as long as possible while at the same time pointing your feet and stretching your legs to make them as long as possible. Do not lift your arms or legs off the floor. Hold the body stretch for 10 seconds. Relax and repeat.

The stretch: Abdomen, front of hips, legs, and underarms.

18. Cobra Stretch

Starting position: Lie flat on your stomach with your hands directly underneath your shoulders, hands turned inward or forward. Rest your forehead on the floor.

Variation: Stretch only one arm and one leg at a time on the same side of the body to give more stretch to the sides of the trunk. Alternate right side and left side.

Stretch one arm and opposite leg simultaneously to give a diagonal stretch. Alternate right and left diagonal stretches.

Action: Using your arms for support, raise your head and chest upward until you feel a stretch in the front of your abdomen. Hold the stretch for 10 seconds. Slowly lower yourself by first lowering your abdomen, then your chest, and finally your head. Relax and repeat.

The stretch: Front of the neck, chest, and abdomen.

Variation: Raise up until your elbows are fully extended. This advanced variation is only for the very limber.

Comments: This exercise, derived from the Yoga "cobra" position, stretches the abdominal muscles while at the same time putting the spine into severe hyper-extension. *It is not for everyone.* This should not be done by anyone who has a history of "back trouble."

19. Standing Side Bend

Starting position: Stand with your feet shoulder width apart, hands clasped together and behind your head.

Action: Keep your head between your arms, and slowly bend as far as you can to one side. Keep your chest facing forward at all times. Hold position 15 seconds. Slowly return to the starting position. Relax and repeat to the other side.

The stretch: The side of the trunk opposite to the direction of the bend. (If your arms swing over to the right side, you are stretching the muscles on the left side of the trunk.)

Variation: To make this exercise a little harder, clasp both hands behind your neck when you lean to the side.

To make this exercise a little easier, keep both hands at your sides instead of overhead. When you lean over, let your hand slide down the outside of your leg for support.

Comments: When you lean over you are stretching muscles along the side of the trunk. When you return to the upright position, the same muscles work to raise your trunk. Therefore, in this exercise you can stretch and strengthen the same muscles.

20. Sitting Trunk Rotation

Starting position: Sit on the floor with one leg straight and the other leg bent and tucked over the straight knee.

Action: Turn your trunk, including shoulders and head, in the opposite direction to the way your leg was crossed over. Hold the position for 10 seconds. Return to the starting position. Repeat to the opposite side.

The stretch: Abdomen and side of the trunk opposite to the turn of the upper body. (If your upper body is turned to the right, you will feel the stretch on the left.)

Progressions: If you have difficulty, bend your elbow and use it as a brace to push against the bent leg as you turn away from it.

21. Standing Trunk Rotation

Starting position: Stand with your back to a wall, your heels approximately 12 inches from the wall. Keep your elbows bent and your hands in front of your shoulders.

Action: Keep your feet in place and turn your head, shoulders and upper body as far as you can toward the wall. Hold this rotated position for 10 seconds. Return to the starting position. Relax and repeat to the opposite side.

The stretch: Abdomen and side of the trunk opposite to the direction of the turn.

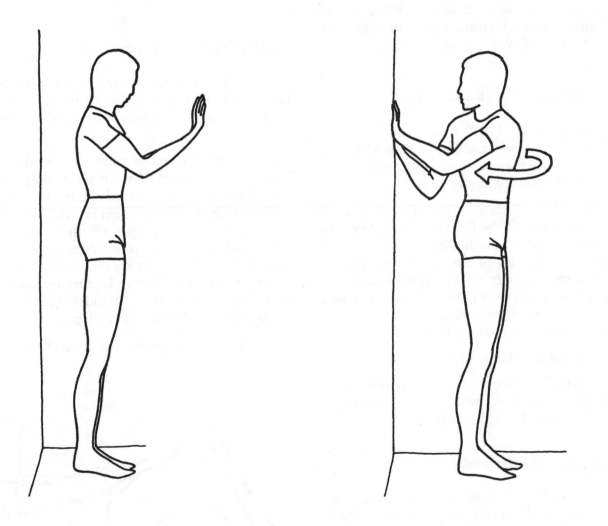

CATEGORY: STRENGTHENING

Special Instructions

If you failed physical fitness tests 1 or 2 and 3 or only 3, start your Basic Program with abdominal strengthening exercises 22a, 22b and 23. When you feel that you are making improvements, then gradually add 26, 27 and 28. Do not do any other exercise in this region until you can perform all of these easily.

If you passed tests 1, 2, and 3 with ease, omit abdominal strengthening exercises 22a, 22d and 23. Proceed with any of the others.

22. Head Raise (a) (Remedial)

Starting position: Lie flat on your back with your knees bent over a pillow or bent with your feet flat on the floor. Use no pillow under your head. Your arms are at your side.

Action: Inhale through your nose, then *raise only your head* off the floor while you blow the air toward your stomach. Exhale through your mouth, blowing all of the air out completely before lowering your head to the starting position. Be sure that your head is tucked down, your chin toward your chest as you curl forward. Uncurl slowly and repeat.

Muscular work: Abdomen and front of the neck.

Comments: To relax your head in between each head raise, roll your head gently from side to side when it rests on the floor.

Head Raise (b) (Remedial)

Starting position: Lie on your back with both knees bent and both feet flat on the floor. Use no pillow under your head. Your arms are at your sides.

Action: Inhale while your head is on the floor and blow the air out through your mouth as you curl forward. *Raise your head, neck, and shoulder blades* off the floor. You may raise your palms a few inches from the floor. Keep your chin tucked down throughout the curling forward. To return to the starting position, uncurl by lowering first your shoulder blades, then your shoulders, and finally your head. Repeat.

Muscular work: Abdomen and front of neck.

Comments: As in Head Raise (a).

23. Partial Sit-Up (Remedial)

Starting position: Lie on your back with your knees bent and both feet flat on the floor. Place your hands on your thighs. Use no pillow under your head.

Action: Inhale through your nose while your head is on the floor. Blow air out through your mouth as you curl forward. Start the curl by tucking your chin down, then raising your head, shoulders and upper back off the floor. Your hands slide up toward your knees as your back curls off the floor. Curl up only until your fingertips reach your knees. Uncurl by lowering your back, then your shoulder blades, and finally your head to the floor. Repeat.

Muscular work: Abdomen and front of the neck.

24. Full Sit-Up

Starting position: Lie on your back with both knees bent and feet flat on the floor. Clasp your hands behind your head. Use no pillow under your head.

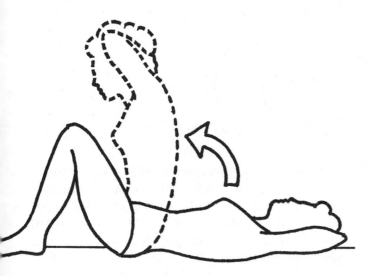

Action: Inhale through your nose when your head is on the floor and exhale through your mouth as you curl forward. Come up to a full sitting position. Uncurl slowly (more slowly than you curled forward), first lowering your lower back, mid-back, upper back and shoulders, and finally your head to the floor.

Muscular work: Abdomen, front of hips, and front of neck.

Progression: Keep your arms crossed on your chest if you find it too difficult to keep them behind your head. You may also hook your feet under a piece of heavy furniture such as a sofa.

Doing this does not detract from the benefit of the exercise.

Comments: If you find that you have to really jerk your body forward to come up, then you should be using an easier version for sit-up exercising such as exercises 22 or 23. This exercise is most beneficial when you can curl forward and uncurl in a slow, controlled manner, no matter which arm position you are using.

25. Rotated Sit-Ups

All variations of sit-ups should be done in the standard position as well as the rotated position. This encourages use of the vertical abdominal fibers and the oblique abdominal fibers.

If your hands are in front of you, place them both to the same side of your thighs when you curl forward. If your hands are crossed on your chest or behind your neck, turn to point one elbow toward the opposite knee *before* you curl up. Stay in the rotated position during the curl-up phase *and* the uncurl phase.

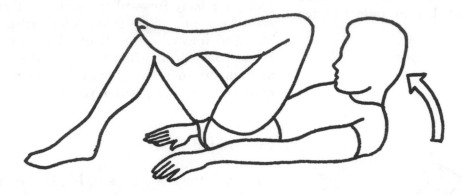

26. Knee-Kiss (Remedial)

Starting position: Lie on your back with both knees bent, feet flat on the floor.

Action: Raise your head and one knee at the same time, trying to get your forehead and knee to touch. Return your head, then your knee, to the starting position. Alternate raising the right knee and the left knee. Repeat slowly and rhythmically.

Muscular work: Abdomen and front of the neck.

Comments: Don't be concerned if your forehead and knee do not touch. The important thing is that you raise your head, shoulders, and upper back as directed. It helps to blow air toward your knee as you raise up, to remind yourself not to hold your breath.

Make sure that you always clear your shoulder blades from the floor. If your knee and forehead touch before the blades clear, then perform the exercise without bringing your knee up as high. This makes the upper body do more work.

27. Pelvic Tilt (Remedial)

Starting position: Lie on your back with both knees bent, both feet flat on the floor.

Before you begin the action of this exercise, place one hand underneath your lower back in the hollow space between your back and the floor. This is called the "lumbar curve." The purpose of this exercise is to reduce the curve by flattening this portion of your back. This is accomplished by contracting your abdominal muscles, a motion that rolls your pelvis backward slightly.

Action: Stay in the starting position. Pull in your abdomen and at the same time lift your buttocks about one-half inch from the floor. The combination of these two movements should give you the feeling that your pelvis is rolling backward and that your lumbar spine is pressing into the floor. Be sure that your spine makes contact with the floor. It is a common mistake to lift it off the floor. Maintain this tilted position for 5 seconds. Try the movement a few times. Place your hand underneath your back again while you are performing the exercise to feel if you are increasing the pressure on your hand. If you are, then you are probably doing the exercise correctly.

Muscular work: Abdomen and buttocks.

Another way to determine if you are effectively tilting your pelvis backward is to place your fingertips lightly on your "hip bones" on the front of your pelvis. If you do the exercise properly, you should feel the bones roll underneath your fingers when you contract the abdominal muscles.

Variations: When you're able to produce the backward tilt using the combination of abdomen and buttock lift, eliminate the buttock lift and do it entirely from the abdominal muscles. This is an excellent exercise to do throughout the day. It can be done in the sitting and standing positions with your knees slightly bent.

Comments: No amount of huffing and puffing or filling your chest with air will take the place of using your abdominal muscles to perform this small but very important movement.

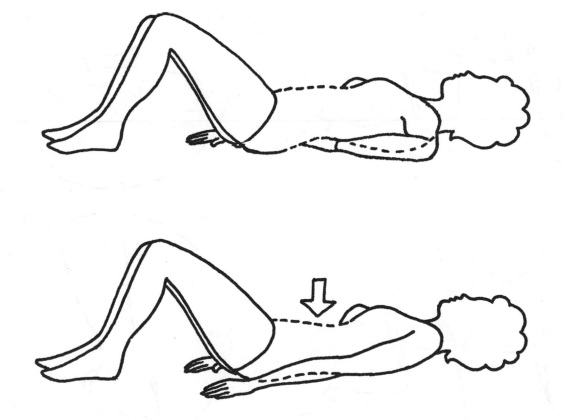

28. Cat Back (Remedial)

Starting position: Assume a hands and knees position on the floor. Your hands should be directly underneath your shoulders and your knees directly underneath your hips. Keep your elbows fully extended. Use hand position (a). If you cannot assume (a) comfortably, use hand position (b).

Action: This exercise has two phases. *Phase one:* Pull in your abdomen to raise your back toward the ceiling. Keep your head down and hold this position for 5 seconds. This phase is like the arching upward of a cat's back. *Phase two:* Lift your head upward at the same time that you let your back sink into a concave curve. Maintain this position for 5 seconds. Repeat, alternating phases.

Muscular work: Abdomen.

Comments: If you experience any back pain in phase two of this exercise, eliminate this part of the exercise.

Remember to keep your elbows fully extended throughout both phases of this exercise.

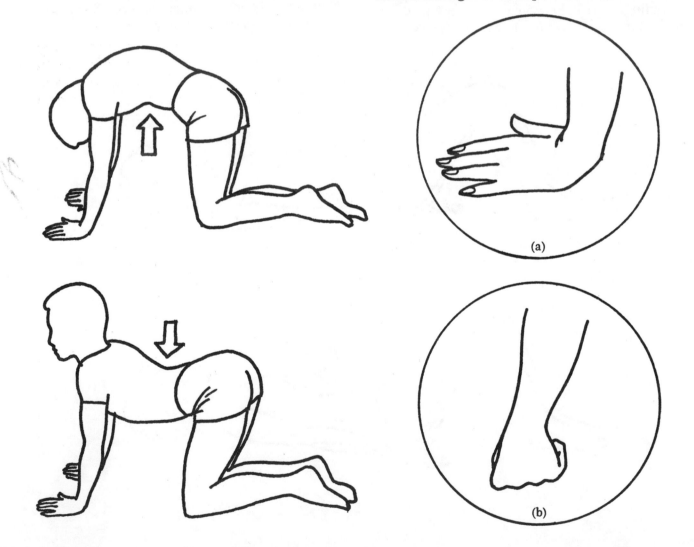

(a)

(b)

29. Double Knee Roll (not illustrated)

Starting position: Lie on your back with both knees bent and raised in the air, directly over your hips. Keep your feet high off the floor.

Action: Keeping your feet off the floor, roll both knees together to one side to touch the floor. Slowly roll your knees to the opposite side to touch the floor. Keep your shoulders on the floor at all times. Repeat, alternating sides.

Muscular work: Lower abdomen.

Comments: If your knees do not roll all the way to the floor, go as far as you can. Go only to the point where your shoulders stay on the floor. If your shoulders and hips roll over together, then all you did was roll over on your side, which doesn't do much for your abdominals.

30. Alternate Elbow Touch (Most difficult)

Starting position: Lie on your back with both knees bent high in the air and with both feet off the floor. Both hands are clasped behind your head and your upper back is off the floor.

Action: Keeping everything off the floor as indicated, bring one elbow and the opposite knee together. Then lower that knee a little and raise the opposite elbow and knee together. The alternating leg action is almost like pedalling in the air with your feet. Slowly and rhythmically alternate knee touching from right to left.

Muscular work: Abdomen.

Progression: To make this exercise more difficult, straighten each leg further and further out until it is parallel with the floor when it is in the lowered position. To develop strength and power, do this exercise more quickly. Alternate as rapidly as you can for 30 seconds.

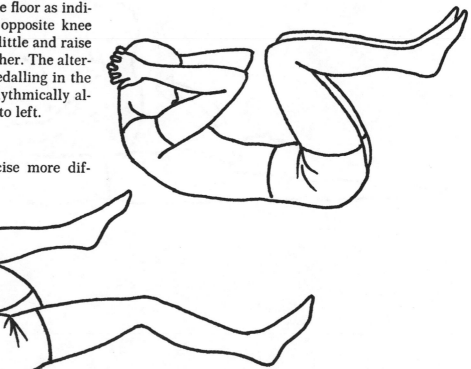

31. Ankle Grasp (Most difficult)

Starting position: Lie flat on your back with both arms outstretched overhead on the floor, both legs straight.

Action: Simultaneously raise your hands to reach for your ankles and draw your knees up toward your chest. Do this in a smooth, controlled manner. Hold the ankle grasping position for a few moments. To return to your original position, keep holding on to your ankles and roll backward until your back is flat on the floor. After your back is flat, let go of your ankles, let your feet touch the floor, and slide the legs back to the straight position. It is very important that you return to the starting position in this manner. If you return the same way you came up, with both back and legs off the floor at the same time, there is excessive stress on the lower back.

Muscular work: Upper and lower abdomen.

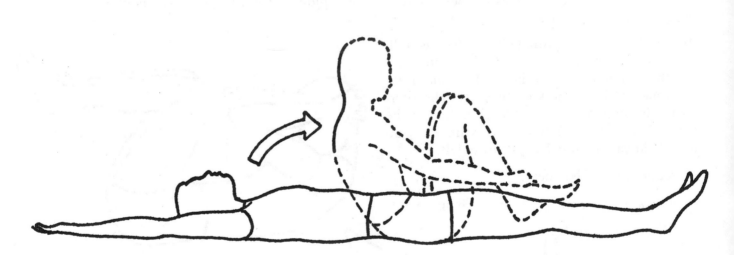

32. Side Trunk Raise (Most difficult)

Starting position: Lie on your side with both legs straight. You will need a partner to hold down your ankles unless there is a belt attached to one end of your exercise table that your feet can loop into. Cross your arms on your chest.

Action: Slowly raise your head and upper trunk. Slowly return to the starting position. Stay on your side throughout the exercise. Repeat for each side.

Muscular work: Uppermost side of trunk.

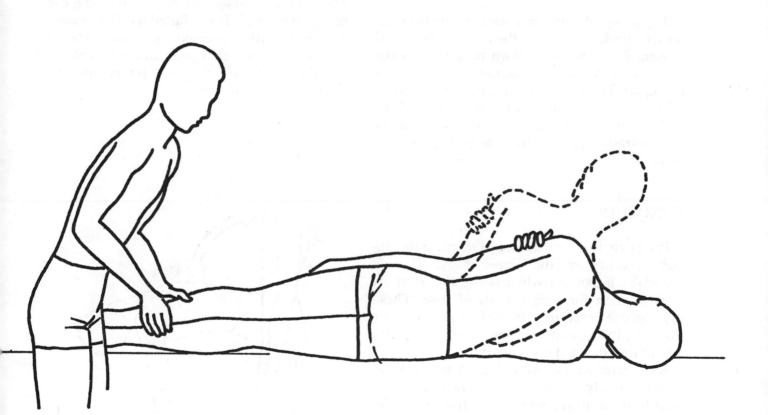

15 || Region IV—Trunk (Extension)

ANATOMY

The group of muscles known as the back extensors are located along the sides of the spinal column from the neck down to the top of the pelvis. Contraction of these muscles straightens the upper body from a forward bent position. When the body is rotated by contraction of the abdominal muscles, the back extensors must be able to stretch sufficiently to permit the body to turn.

FUNCTION

Back extensor strength helps stabilize the upright posture of the upper body. This is especially important when skiing in a forward bent position for long periods of time. These muscles are constantly at work to prevent your upper body from succumbing totally to gravity and falling forward completely.

Back extensor flexibility allows you to bend forward freely without restrictive stiffness in your back. It allows you to take tumbles in the snow in a more relaxed manner, an important aspect of injury prevention.

Special Instructions

If you failed physical fitness tests 6 and 8, start your Basic Program with back extensor stretch, Sitting Bend, 33, and Rotated Sitting Bend, 34, as well as hamstring stretching exercises, Chapter 17. If you failed test 6, but passed 8, concentrate more on the back extensor stretches. Be sure that you can do the remedial exercises easily before you attempt any other stretches in this region.

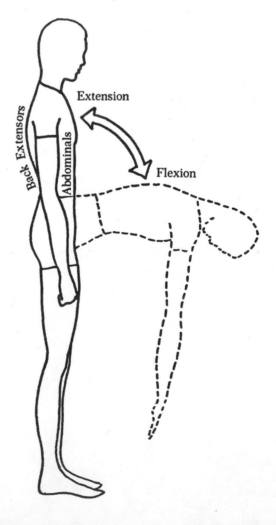

CATEGORY: STRETCHING

33. Sitting Bend (Remedial)

Starting position: Sit on the edge of a firm chair with both.feet on the floor, knees spread apart slightly.

Action: Let your head droop toward your chest. Continue rolling your shoulders and upper body forward until your fingertips touch the floor between your feet. It helps to exhale while you roll downward. Let your body be very loose and floppy. Do not strain to reach the floor. Hold each forward bent stretch for 15 seconds. To sit up, pull in your abdomen and uncurl segmentally. First raise your mid-back, then upper back, shoulders, neck, and finally your head. Relax and repeat.

The stretch: Along spine from neck to low back.

Variation: If you find that this stretch is too much for you, keep your hands on your knees as you bend over. Lower yourself just enough to touch your chest to your knees and control your descent with your hands for support. Or, place one, two, or three pillows in your lap to accommodate your stiffness. As your muscles become more limber, decrease the number of pillows.

34. Rotated Sitting Bend (Remedial)

Starting position: Sit on the edge of a firm chair with both feet on the floor, knees spread apart slightly. Place one hand behind your back and the other hand on the outside of the opposite knee.

Action: Roll downward as you exhale, letting your fingertips reach toward the outside of your foot. Hold this stretched position for 15 seconds. Uncurl by pulling in your abdomen and rolling up segmentally: first your mid-back, upper back, shoulders, neck, and finally your head. Reverse your hands and repeat to the other side after a brief pause.

The stretch: Side and back of the trunk opposite to the turning direction.

Variations: See Variations, exercise 33.

35. Total Body Roll

Starting position: Lie on your back, raise your knees toward your chest, and grasp just below both knees with your hands. Keep your chin tucked down.

Action: Roll your body as one unit forward and backward in the tucked position.

The stretch: Upper back, mid-back, and between the shoulder blades.

Comments: This exercise can be used at any time during an exercise session for intermittent relaxation.

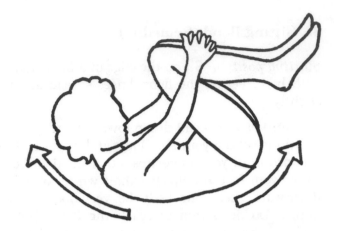

36. Counter-Rotated Body Twist

Starting position: Lie on your back with one knee bent and the other knee straight. Tuck the foot of the bent knee under the knee of the straight leg. This causes your hips to roll over in the same direction as the bent knee.

Action: Keep your bent knee where it is. Turn your head, raise your arm, and stretch it on a diagonal on the floor. Keep your head turned to look at your outstretched hand. Hold this stretched position for 15 seconds. Relax and repeat to the other side by reversing the leg and arm positions.

The stretch: Along the side of the trunk, upper back, and underside of the outstretched arm.

Variation: Increase the stretch for the underside of the arm by holding a small weight (approximately 2 or 3 pounds) in your outstretched hand. Do this on a bed so that the weight hangs over the edge of the bed.

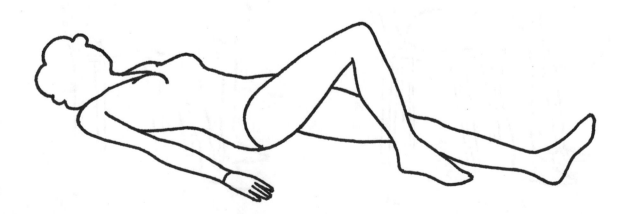

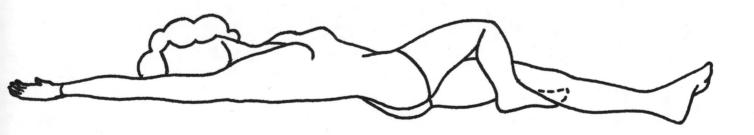

37. Backward Roll Over (Most difficult)

Starting position: Lie on your back.

Action: Bend your knees, raise them in the air and roll them up in the air until they come to rest on your forehead. Keep your hands on your lower back or buttocks for support. Once you feel comfortable, lower your hands to the floor. Hold this position to stretch for 30 seconds.

Slowly lower your legs to the starting position before repeating.

The stretch: Along entire spine from neck to lower back.

Variations: After touching your knees to your forehead, let your knees drop down to the level of your ears. If you are also very limber in the back of your legs, straighten your knees and touch your toes to the floor above your head.

38. Standing Floor Touch (Do not do this exercise unless you are comfortable with Sitting Bend exercise)

Starting position: Stand with feet about shoulder width apart.

Action: Drop your head down toward your chest, and roll your shoulders and upper body toward the floor. Let your fingertips hang loosely toward the floor. *Do not strain to reach the floor.* Stretch in this position for 30 seconds. Please refer to Instructions for Stretching for specific procedure. *To come back up to standing, first bend both knees, pull in your abdomen, and then uncurl your upper body to stand.*

The stretch: Along the spine from upper back to lower back and along the back of both legs.

Variation: If you are more than 10 inches from the floor with your fingertips, place a pile of books on the floor and start by resting your fingers on them while you hold the stretch.

Comments: Never come up to the standing position from the forward bent position with your knees straight. If you do, excessive stress is placed on the structures of the lower back.

Special Instructions

If you failed tests 4 and/or 5, start with back extensor strengthening exercise 39 for your Basic Program. Add other strengthening exercises in this region only when you can do this exercise easily.

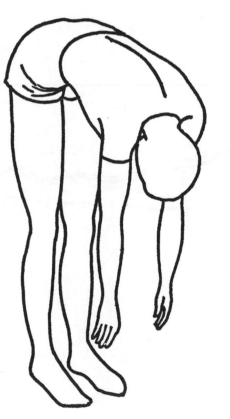

CATEGORY: STRENGTHENING

39. Alternate Arm and/or Leg Lift (Remedial)

Starting position: Lie on your stomach with a large pillow underneath your abdomen and hips, your head resting on the floor. The pillow should be large enough to make you feel that your body is rounded over it, with your head and feet lower than your buttocks. Stretch both arms straight out ahead of you on the floor, and keep both legs straight.

Action: Raise one arm off the floor. Raise only enough to clear your arm completely of floor contact. Hold this raised position for 5 seconds.

Lower and repeat with the opposite arm. Repeat the same procedure one leg at a time.

Muscular work: Upper back, lower back, and buttocks.

Variation: Raise one arm and the opposite leg to the horizontal position at the same time.

Comments: Your goal is to lift and hold the position with your body as elongated as possible. You are *not* to try to raise your arms or legs as high in the air as your possibly can. Doing this would create excessive arching in your lower back.

40. Upper Back Lift

Starting position: Lie on your stomach with a large pillow underneath your abdomen and hips, your head resting on the floor. The pillow should be large enough to make you feel that your body is rounded over it, with your head and feet lower than your buttocks. Use two pillows if necessary. Have someone hold your feet down or hook them under a piece of heavy furniture.

Action: Keep your hands at your sides or tucked underneath your thighs and raise your head and chest off the floor. (Do not use your hands to lift your trunk off the floor.) *Lift only until your upper body is parallel with the floor.* Hold this position for 5 seconds. Lower slowly and repeat.

Muscular work: Mid and lower back.

Progressions: Keep both hands clasped behind your head instead of at your sides; or keep both arms outstretched ahead of you with your head between your arms. The most difficult version is to do any of the lift positions without any support holding down your ankles.

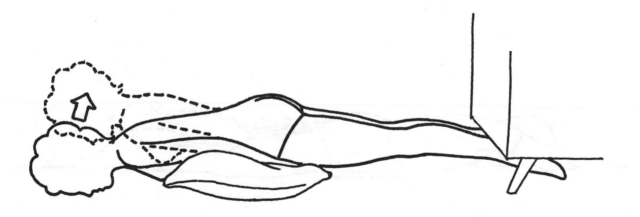

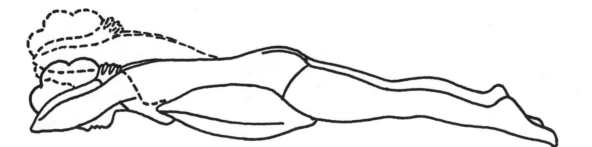

41. Double Leg Lift

Starting position: Lie on your stomach with a large pillow underneath your abdomen and hips, your head resting on your arms or on the floor. The pillow should be large enough to make you feel that your body is rounded over it and that your head and feet are lower than your buttocks.

Action: Keep your legs straight and raise them both off the floor at the same time. (Do not raise your upper body at all.) Raise your legs until your thighs, and the entire leg, is clear of all floor contact. Hold this position for 5 seconds. Lower and repeat.

Muscular work: Lower back, buttocks, and back of thighs.

Variation: If you have minor difficulty with this exercise, hold onto a piece of heavy furniture with both hands when you do the leg lift. Keep the pillow underneath your belly.

16 || Region V—Front of Thigh, Including Front of Hip Joint (Knee Extension and Hip Flexion)

ANATOMY

The muscles in the front of the hip produce hip flexion (iliopsoas muscle) and knee extension (quadriceps muscle). (Hip extension and knee flexion will be described in Chapters 21 and 17.) The hip flexor, located deep in the pelvis, arises from the vertebrae of the lower back and attaches to the inside of the thigh bone (femur). Contraction of this muscle brings your thigh toward your torso.

The muscles of knee extension, the quadriceps, make up the bulk of the front of the thigh. They arise from the pelvis and thigh bone and attach as a broad tendon over the kneecap (patella). Contractions of the quadriceps bring the knee from a bent (flexed) to a straight (extended) position. In addition, gradual, controlled lengthening of the quadriceps allows you to slowly bend your knees from the standing position. This type of muscular strength is used constantly in downhill skiing.

FUNCTION

Good hip flexion is needed for an assertive leg drive in cross-country technique. Good flexibility allows the rear leg to extend well back after the kick. Downhill maneuvers that involve lifting the ski upward off the snow usually require good, strong, quick hip flexion.

The most important function of the quadriceps in skiing is to maintain the skier's legs in a partially bent position. Flexibility exercises for the quadriceps are important for releasing the tension that comes with the prolonged muscular shortening when the muscles are frequently used.

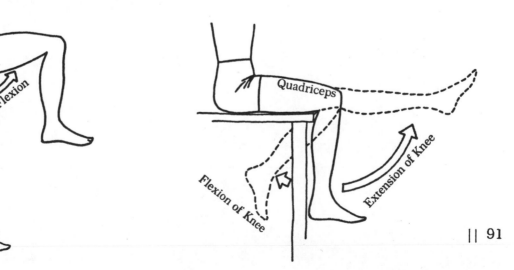

CATEGORY: STRETCHING

Special Instructions

Stretching exercises in Region V include stretches for the muscles of hip flexion as well as knee extension. Therefore, you must include both types of exercises:

Exercise 42 or 43 and

Exercise 44 or 45 or 46

If you failed physical fitness test 7, start your Basic Program with hip flexor stretching exercises 42 and 43.

42. Hip Flexor Stretch, Backlying (Remedial)
(For illustration see Physical Fitness Test 7)

Starting position: Lie on your back on the bed with both knees bent as close as possible to your chest. Hold your knees in this position with your hands. Your feet should be very close to the edge of the bed.

Action: Hold one knee tightly toward your chest with both hands interlocked below the knee; let the other leg drop down to dangle over the edge of the bed. Allow the dangling leg to drop as far as possible without moving the upper one at all. Hold this position of stretch for 30 seconds.

The stretch: In the front of the dangling hip.

Variation: You can help the stretching procedure if you have another person to work with you. The other person stands in front of your dangling leg, which is not yet at its lowest point. He places his hands on your thigh, just above your knee.

You attempt to pull your knee up toward the ceiling while your partner resists the motion by pushing downward with his hands. His resistance should equal your pulling force so that there is no movement. Hold this isometric position for 10 seconds, then immediately but gently lower your dangling leg further than before with your partner's light assistance.

43. Standing Hip Flexor Stretch

Starting position: Stand with one leg ahead of the other. The knee of the front leg is flexed to a right angle and the foot is flat on the floor. Put the other leg far behind you, resting only on the forefoot. Both feet should point forward, and your hips should face forward at all times.

Action: With your hands on your hips, keep your feet in the same position and lower your body slightly by letting the front knee bend more. If you feel no stretch in the front of the rear leg, then you should place your rear leg further back. Hold this position of stretch for 30 seconds. Relax and repeat with the other leg forward.

The stretch: Front of the hip of the rear leg.

Variation: You can produce a similar stretch by placing your front foot on the edge of a chair seat.

Comments: Be sure to keep your upper body erect. Lower your entire body as a unit. Keep your hips facing forward at all times during the stretch. Keep your hands on your hips as a reminder.

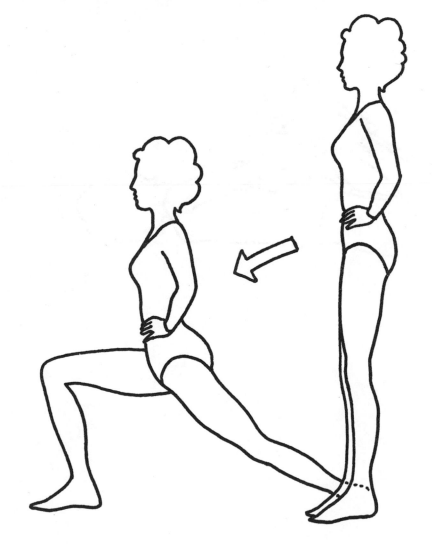

44. Double Front Thigh Stretch

Starting position: Lie on your stomach and grasp each ankle with your hands.

Action: Use your hands to pull your feet toward your buttocks. Keep your thighs on the floor at all times.

The stretch: Front of the thighs.

Comments: If you have had any problems with your knees, check with your doctor before pulling your feet back as far as you can. In some cases, extreme knee flexion can aggravate a pre-existing knee condition.

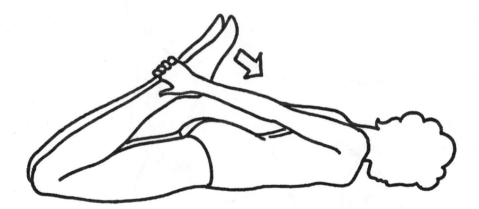

45. Side-Lying Thigh Stretch

Starting position: Lie on your side with your bottom leg bent slightly, your head resting comfortably, and grasp your top ankle with your hand.

Action: Keep your knee at the same level as your hip (do not lift your knee toward the ceiling), and pull your thigh straight backward with your hand. If your back begins to arch, you have pulled your leg too far. Stretch for 15 seconds. Relax and repeat.

The stretch: Front of the thigh.

Progression: To add more stretch to the hip and thigh raise your knee higher in the air, then extend your foot as far as your arm's length will allow.

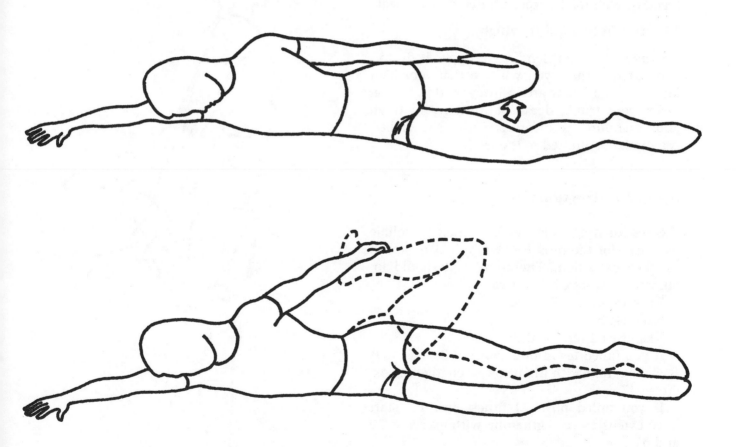

46. Standing Front Thigh Stretch

Starting position: Stand on one leg with your hand holding the foot of the free leg. If necessary, hold on to the back of a chair or countertop for balance.

Action: Use your hand to pull your leg backward. Keep both thighs parallel to each other. (There is a tendency for the bent knee to drift out toward the side.) Keep your upper body erect. Stretch for 15 seconds. Relax and repeat.

The stretch: Front of the thigh.

Comments: If you bend your upper body forward at the waist, you will see that your bent knee does go backward. However, this motion flexes your trunk, does not stretch your thigh and, therefore, is incorrect form. Remember, the motion is limited to the leg.

Special Instructions

Strengthening exercises in Region V include exercises for the muscles of hip flexion as well as knee extension. Therefore, you should include both types of exercises.

Exercise 47 or 48
Exercise 50
Exercise 51 (optional)

If you failed test 1 or 2, but not 3, start your Basic Program with hip flexor strengthening exercise 47.

If you failed physical fitness test 11, start knee extension strengthening with exercises 50 and 51.

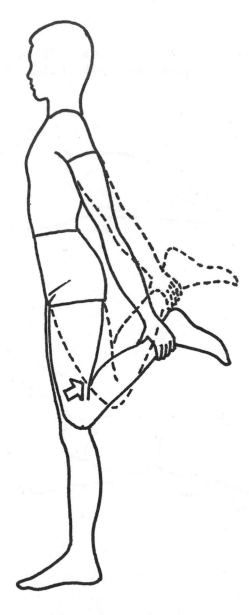

CATEGORY: STRENGTHENING

47. Rotated Leg Raise

Starting position: Lie on your back with one leg bent, foot flat on the floor and the other leg straight on the floor.

Action: Turn the straight leg outward (external rotation) and slowly raise it as high as you can. Lower your leg to the starting position and repeat.

Muscular work: Front of hip and thigh.

Progression: Add light weights to the ankle, starting with 2 pounds.

Variation: Leg Raise, Straight. This exercise emphasizes both knee extension and hip flexion. Follow the same starting position as above, but when you begin the action of lifting, do not turn your leg outward. Keep your toes and kneecap facing toward the ceiling at all times and keep your knee fully extended. Add weights to the ankle as above to progress.

Comments: If your leg is going high in the air but your knee bends during the last part of the Straight Leg Raise exercise, then you are lifting higher than you should. The benefit in this exercise comes with the knee fully extended.

This exercise is frequently used in the rehabilitation of knee injuries.

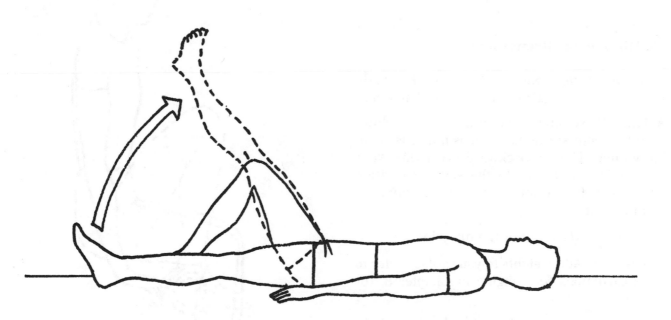

Rotated Leg Raise

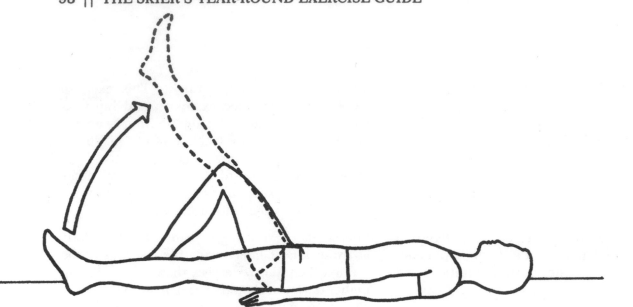

Straight Leg Raise

48. Hip Flexor Strengthener

Starting position: Sit on the edge of a high, padded table or chair with your legs dangling.

Action: Raise one knee toward your chest. Maintain your sitting position as much as possible without leaning backward every time your knee is raised. Lower to the starting position and repeat. Lower your knee more slowly than you raised it.

Muscular work: Front of the hip joint.

Progression: Add weights to your ankle. Refer to the Instructions for weights in Chapter 8, for details.

Comments: If you are also doing the sitting knee extension exercise 49 with weights, you can do this exercise from the same sitting position. Be sure to vary the weight appropriately if each exercise requires a different number of pounds.

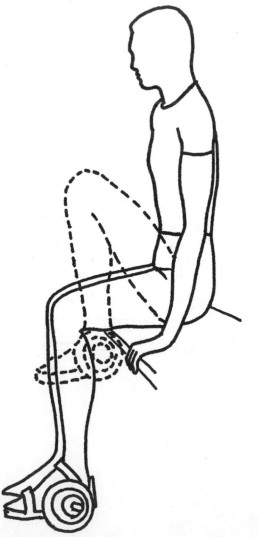

49. Quadriceps Setting, Isometric (Rehabilitation)

Starting position: Sit on a bed with your leg fully extended and a small, rolled towel underneath your knee.

Action: Tighten your thigh and your kneecap and maintain the tension for 5 seconds. Relax then repeat. (It helps to try to push the back of your knee down into the towel at the same time.) When you contract your quadriceps mus-cle, your heel may rise off of the bed, which is acceptable.

Muscular work: Front of the thigh and kneecap.

Variation: The same isometric contraction of the quadriceps muscle can be done whenever you attempt to extend your knee against an im-movable object. For example, you can face a wall, place your toes against it and apply sus-tained pressure forward as if you were kicking your leg through the wall.

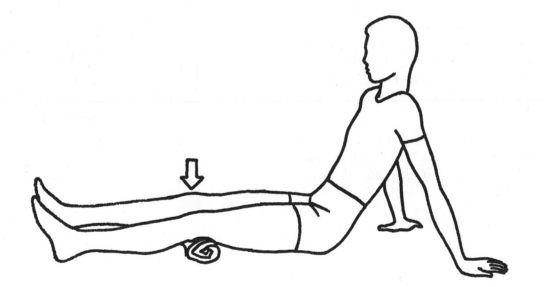

50. Wall Sitting, Isometric (Remedial and most difficult)

Starting position: Stand with your back against a wall and your feet flat on the floor about 1½ to 2 feet from the wall.

Action: Slide your back down the wall until your thighs are parallel with the floor. Your feet should be directly beneath your knees. If they are not, adjust your foot position so that your thighs and lower legs form a right angle. Stay in this position as long as you possibly can.

Muscular work: Front of the thighs.

Variations: Begin with the duration of time that you stayed in this position when you did this for the physical fitness test. Increase the length of time by 10-second increments.

If you did this for 30 seconds or less, start practicing with your hips higher than your knees and gradually work up to the point where you can perform 30 seconds in the standard position, hips level with knees; then work on increasing your total time in the standard position.

Comments: This exercise is easier to practice if you are barefoot or wear non-skid shoes or sneakers. Use a wall that isn't too slick when you first start out.

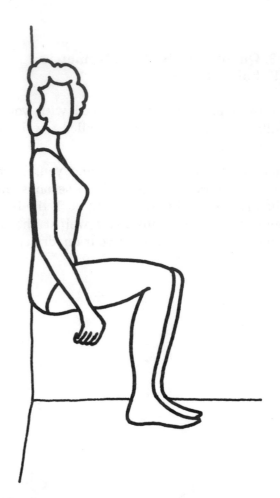

51. Knee Extension, Sitting

Starting position: Sit on the edge of a high table with both legs dangling freely. Place a small towel underneath each knee to pad the table's edge.

Action: Raise one foot in the air until your knee is fully extended. Keep your thigh in contact with the tabletop at all times. Take 2 to 3 seconds to raise the leg and about 4 to 6 seconds to lower it.

Muscular work: Front of the thigh.

Comments: There should be a weight on your foot. Start with 5 pounds of weight unless you are recovering from an injury, in which case you will start with 1 or 2 pounds. If you have had an injury, please refer to Chapter 33, Rehabilitation Exercises. Use the amount of weight that enables you to extend your knee 10 times. You should be able to complete all 10 repetitions in good form, working hard to complete the last few of the 10.

If you cannot complete the full extension (but you could without any weight), or if you have to swing your entire leg violently to get it extended, you are using too much weight.

Warm up first by doing a few repetitions with half your usual amount of weight.

Do 3 sets of 10 repetitions each for each leg. Alternate right and left sets to give each leg a chance to relax in between sets.

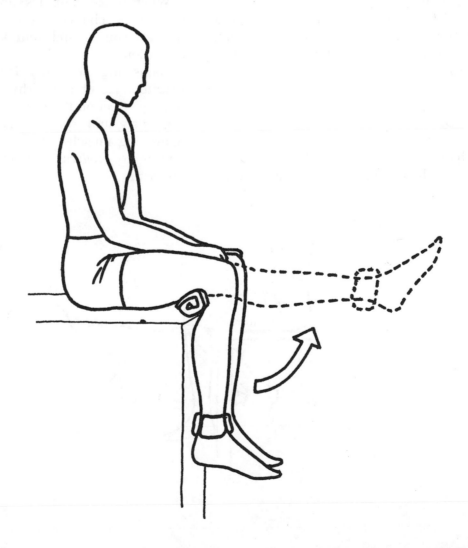

17 || Region VI—Back of Thigh (Knee Flexion)

ANATOMY

The muscles of knee flexion are the hamstrings. They are located in the back of the thigh, arising from the back of the pelvis and attaching behind the knee joint.

Contraction of the hamstrings brings your foot toward your buttock. Good strength provides protection to the structures around the knee joint.

FUNCTION

Good hamstring strength enables you to unweight the tails of your skis more effectively if you are actually raising them off the snow. You can respond more quickly and ski more aggressively in uneven terrain.

When these muscles are easily stretched, there is less chance of a severe strain if your ski tip gets caught and your knee is sprung into extension.

Hamstring flexibility is important for the maintenance of a healthy back because of its pulling effect on the pelvis.

Cyclists and runners have unusually tight hamstring muscles and should pay special attention to progressive stretches in their basic program.

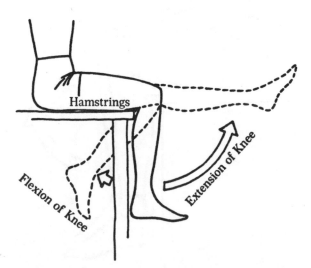

CATEGORY: STRETCHING

Special Instructions

If you failed physical fitness test 6 and/or 8 you should start your hamstring stretches with Aerial Hamstring Stretch, 52, Single Leg Hamstring Stretch, 53, and Special Remedial Hamstring Stretch, 54. Be sure you can do these comfortably before trying other stretches in this region.

Also, refer to Chapter 15, exercise 38, Standing Floor Touch, which stretches hamstrings in addition to back extensors. Be sure to keep a progress record of the distance (in inches) that your fingertips are from the floor.

52. Aerial Hamstring Stretch (Remedial)

Starting position: Lie on your back with both knees bent and both feet flat on the floor.

Action: Step 1: Bend one knee toward your chest.

Step 2: Raise your foot toward the ceiling until your knee is completely extended. If you have to lower your leg to get the knee straight, do so. Hold your leg in this stretched position for 5 seconds.

Step 3: Lower the straight leg to the floor, then return it to the starting position. Alternate right and left legs.

The stretch: Behind the thigh and knee.

Variations: Point your heel to the ceiling when your leg is fully extended.

Point your toes to the ceiling when your leg is fully extended.

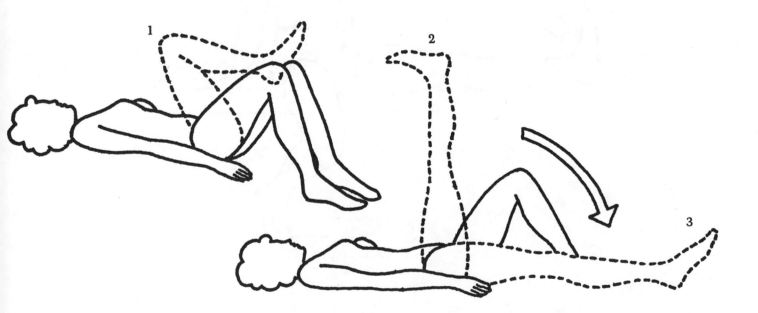

53. Single Leg Hamstring Stretch (Remedial)

Starting position: Sit on the edge of a bed or high table so that one leg is out straight on the bed, knee fully extended. The other leg is on the floor or supported by a chair.

Action: Bend the ankle of the extended leg so that your toes point toward the ceiling. Reach forward with your hands toward your ankle. Reach slowly. Remember to breathe and relax while you are stretching. Stretch for 30 seconds. Do not bounce! Relax and repeat.

The stretch: Behind the thigh, knee, and ankle.

Variations: If you cannot reach your ankle, try the following:

Reach toward your knee or however far your hands reach and place your hands on that part of your leg as you stretch.

Hook a towel around the bottom of your foot and hold one end in each hand. Pull yourself forward very gently by the towel. This same towel technique is used as a rehabilitation exercise to stretch the heel cord tendon and calf muscles.

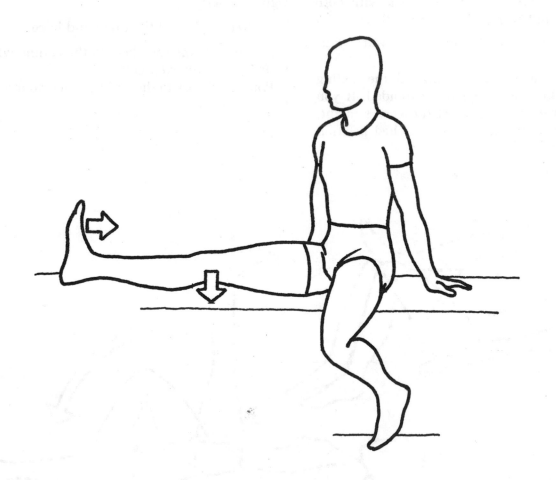

54. Special Remedial Hamstring Stretch

If you are unable to assume the sitting position with one or both of your knees fully extended (that is, your knee pops up as soon as you start to lean forward), you must begin your hamstring stretching with the following exercise.

Starting position: Sit on the edge of a bed or table as instructed in Single Leg Hamstring stretch, 53, with one addition. Be sure to sit with the sole of your foot flat against a wall. You can also use a "half-V" position and sit on the floor as shown in exercise 55.

Action: Lean backward with your upper body and support yourself with your hands. Lean back until you reach the point that you can keep your knee fully extended. From this position, use your hands to rock yourself gently forward to feel the stretch behind your leg. Hold this stretch for 30 seconds. Or, hook a rope around a heavy piece of furniture and gently pull yourself forward with the rope. Relax and repeat.

Comment: The purpose of the exercise is completely defeated once your knee is allowed to bend.

55. V-Spread Hamstring Stretch

Starting position: Sit on the floor with both legs spread into a wide "V"

Action: Keep your ankle bent, with your toes pointing to the ceiling. Lower your head, roll your upper body down, and reach toward one ankle with your hands. Hold the position for 30 seconds at the furthest point your hands can reach, if not to your ankle (knee level, mid-shin, etc.). Return to the starting position before repeating to the other side.

The stretch: Side of the trunk, back of the thigh, and knee.

Variation—The Half-V: Sit with one foot brought in near your groin and the other leg stretched out to the side. Reverse position to stretch the other leg.

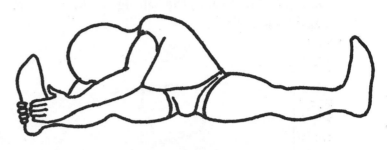

Comments: The bonus of this exercise is a stretch to the back extensors and the inner thigh as well as the back of the thigh and knee. If you passed the Straight Leg Raising test in the Physical Fitness quiz, but you cannot reach your ankle, you may be limited by tightness in your back extensors. You should work on stretching the back extensors before including this exercise in your Basic Program.

If you pass the Straight Leg Raising test and the Fingertips to Floor test, you have ample flexibility in both your back extensors and hamstring muscles. Inability to perform this exercise might be due to tightness in the adductor muscles of the inner thigh. See Chapter 18, stretches of the adductors, Region VII.

56. Double Leg Hamstring Stretch (Most difficult)

Starting position: Sit on the floor with both legs straight, knees fully extended, ankles bent, with toes pointing toward the ceiling and soles of feet against a wall.

Action: Bend forward with your upper body, reaching your hands as far as you can toward your ankles, toes, or farther. Hold the stretch for 30 seconds. Relax and repeat.

The stretch: Behind the neck, mid and lower back, lower buttocks, behind thighs, knees, calves, and ankles.

Comments: If you can reach easily to your ankles without excessive stretching in the back of your legs, but you are unable to keep your feet pointing toward the ceiling, you may be limited only by shortening of the calf muscles. Refer to Chapter 22 for calf stretching exercises.

57. Standing Hamstring Stretch

Starting position: Stand with one leg fully extended and supported on a table.

Action: Place your hands on your knee for support and gently lean toward your straight leg. Lean as far as you can without letting the knee bend. Hold the stretch for 30 seconds. Relax and repeat.

The stretch: Behind the thigh and knee of the raised leg.

Variations: Keep both feet pointing in the same direction as illustrated, or pivot the standing foot so that it points out to the side.

Keep the foot of the raised leg pointing toward the ceiling to add a stretch to the calf.

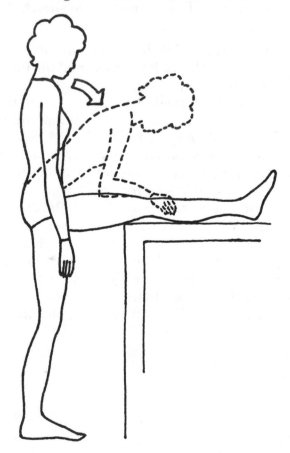

CATEGORY: STRENGTHENING

Special Instructions

Strengthening for Region VI includes both isotonic and isometric exercises. Include them both in your Basic Program. Choose different exercises from time to time to strengthen this muscle group from varying positions: sitting, standing, prone.

58. Prone Knee Flexion, with Weights

Starting position: Lie flat on your stomach with a weight on your ankle. Use a pillow under your abdomen and hips if you have low back discomfort.

Action: Flex one knee to bring your heel as close as possible to your buttock. Slowly lower your foot to the starting position. Lower your foot more slowly than you raised it. Repeat. Follow specific instructions for the use of weights, Chapter 8.

Muscular work: Back of the thigh.

Comments: If you experience discomfort in the front of the thigh when you do this exercise, this may be due to tightness of the quadriceps or hip flexor muscles in the front of the hip and thigh. Be sure to have Region V stretches, Chapter 16, in your Basic Program to reduce this tightness.

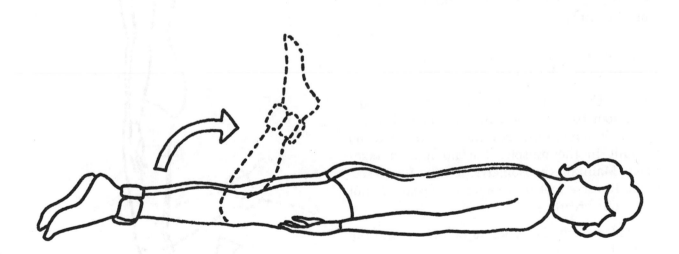

59. Standing Knee Flexion, with Weights

Starting position: Stand with thighs and feet close together. If necessary, hold lightly onto a countertop or piece of furniture for balance.

Action: Keep your thighs together and flex one knee to raise your foot toward your buttock. Lower your foot more slowly than you raise it. Refer to Chapter 8 for specific details on progressing with weights.

Muscular work: Back of the thigh.

Comments: If you find that you are dipping your upper body forward each time you try to lift the weights all the way up, you are probably using weights that are too heavy.

60. Sitting Knee Flexion, Isometric
(not illustrated)

Starting position: Sit in a firm chair with your feet crossed at the ankles.

Action: Use the front foot to try and pull the other foot back underneath the chair. Use the back foot to resist the movement, so that tension is built in the muscles but no motion takes place. Maintain the isometric tension for 10 seconds. Reverse foot positions and repeat. Do not hold your breath.

Muscular work: The back of one thigh and the front of the other.

Variation: Place your feet further forward or backward to work the muscles in different positions.

Comments: This exercise is an isometric exercise for the hamstring muscles of the leg in front and an isometric exercise for the quadriceps muscles of the leg in back.

This exercise can be done throughout the day at any time that you are sitting at a desk or in any convenient chair.

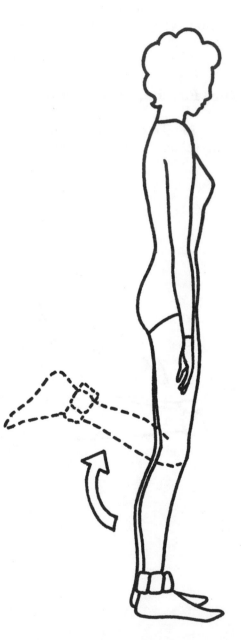

61. Prone Knee Flexion, Isometric

Starting position: Lie flat on your stomach. Flex both knees, with your feet hooked around each other at the ankles. Use a pillow under your abdomen and hips if you have back discomfort.

Action: Use one foot to resist the motion of the other. Try to bring one foot closer to your buttock, but at the same time resist the movement entirely with the other foot. Maintain the isometric tension for 10 seconds. Reverse foot positions and repeat. Remember to continue to breathe normally even though you are vigorously tensing the leg muscles.

Muscular work: Back of one thigh and front of the other.

Variation: Repeat the tensing with the feet at various distances from the floor.

Comments: This is an isometric exercise for the hamstring muscles of one leg and the quadriceps muscles of the opposite leg.

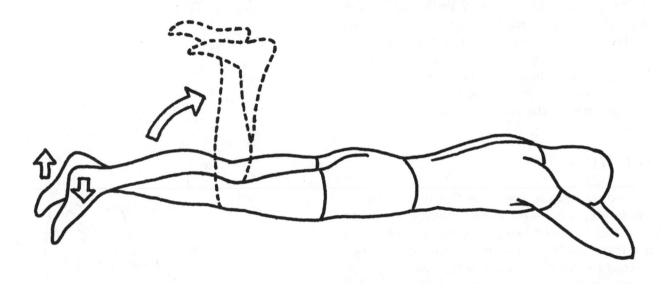

62. Self-Resisted Knee Flexion

Starting position: Use the same starting position as exercise 61 (Prone Knee Flexion, Isometric).

Action: This exercise is isotonic, permitting the legs to develop muscular tension and to move actively. You are to let one foot move slowly toward the floor, but resist the movement with the other foot. The resisting foot should apply as much pressure as possible so that both legs move very slowly. Repeat the same procedure, moving the feet toward the buttocks. Reverse foot positions and repeat sequence.

Muscular work: The front of one thigh and the back of the other.

18 | Region VII—Inner Thigh (Hip Adduction)

ANATOMY

The muscles for adduction are located in the inner thigh. They originate in the inner groin on the pubic bone and along the upper inside of the thigh bone. They attach to the lower inside end of the thigh bone and the knee.

Contraction of the adductor muscles brings your leg toward the center of your body.

FUNCTION

Good strength is needed in the adductor muscles to keep your skis close together, to move the downhill ski in side-stepping, and to move a ski from an outside position in toward the other ski.

Good flexibility is important to avoid serious muscle pulls that may result if you fall with your leg outstretched or caught in the snow to one side of the body.

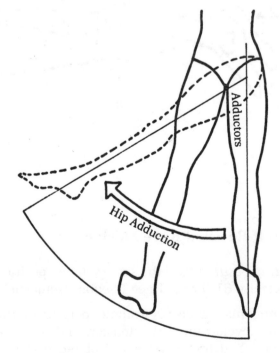

CATEGORY: STRETCHING

Special Instructions

If you failed Physical Fitness Quiz test 10, start your Basic Program with adductor stretches: Adductor Spread, Sitting, 63, and Adductor Spread, Knees Bent, 64. When you have developed a good feel for the stretch of this region, try exercise 65, Adductor Stretch, Standing. Add the other stretches when you can pass test 10 easily.

63. Adductor Spread, Sitting (Remedial and most difficult)

Starting position: Sit on the floor with your legs straddling the corner of a rug, or estimate a right angle position by starting with one leg flush up against a wall.

Action: With your hands behind you, spread your legs as far apart as you can. Gently lean forward with your upper body to increase the stretch in the inner thighs. Keep your knees fully extended at all times. Hold position 30 seconds. Repeat.

The stretch: Inner thighs and groin.

Progression: Start with your hands behind you for balance and assistance in leaning forward. As your muscles become more flexible, place your hands on your thighs, knees, or ankles, or straight out on the floor directly in front of you.

Variation: Sit in position facing a partner, your feet touching your partner's. Both partners hold hands. One partner leans backward very slowly to pull the other person forward, thereby aiding the forward body lean and the adductor stretch. The person receiving the stretch must be the one to determine the distance that he should be pulled forward. Reverse pulling and leaning roles to give a stretch to the other person.

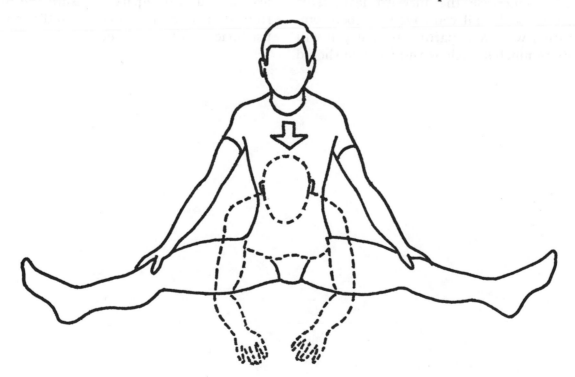

Comments: This is a muscle group that should be stretched very slowly and very carefully to avoid harmful muscle "pulls." Do not bounce or make jerky movements to increase the stretch.

You can have another person stand behind you and very, very gently push your upper body forward to increase the forward lean. This should only be done if you have very good communication with your partner so that you will get only as much stretch as you feel you should have.

Measure your progress in two ways:

1. With your legs spread as far apart as possible, have someone measure the distance between the insides of your ankle bones.

2. Lean forward as far as possible with your legs spread wide apart. Measure the distance from your nose to the floor or to the top of two fists placed in front of you.

64. Adductor Spread, Knees Bent (Remedial)

Starting position: Sit on the floor with both knees bent, the soles of your feet together, and your feet as close to your groin as possible.

Action: For some people, just getting into the starting position is enough of an exercise. Use your hands to push your knees apart and hold them in this position for 15 seconds, or use your hands to pull your feet toward your groin and press your knees apart with your elbows. Relax and repeat.

The stretch: Inner thighs and groin.

Progression: Pull your feet toward your groin, press your knees apart with your elbows, and lean forward with your upper body to increase the stretch.

Comments: If this position creates discomfort in your knees do not use this position for adductor stretching. Choose other exercises from this region.

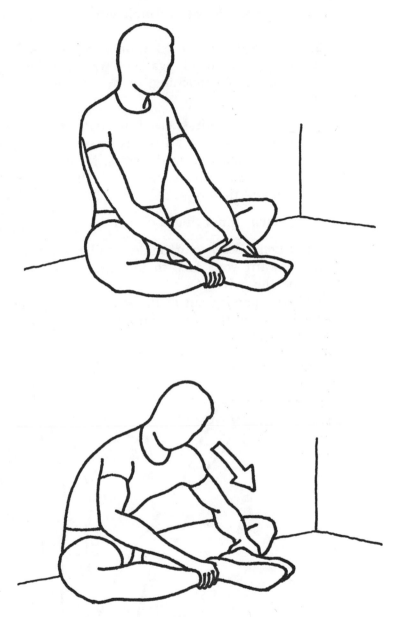

65. Adductor Stretch, Standing
(not illustrated)

Starting position: Stand with your feet more than shoulder width apart. Face straight ahead and keep both feet pointing in the same direction as your nose.

Action: Bend one knee and shift your weight onto that leg. This allows the other leg to straighten out. With your feet still in the starting position you can get a nice stretch of the inside of the straight leg. Maintain this stretch for 15 seconds. Return to the starting position. and repeat to the other side.

The stretch: Inside of the thigh of the straightened leg.

Comments: If you brace the foot of the straightened leg against a wall, you have a more stable position from which to stretch. Wearing rubber soled shoes also helps reduce foot sliding.

This exercise can be done in a ski lodge before putting on your boots and outside in the snow when your boots are on.

66. Adductor Stretch, Backlying

Starting position: Lie on your back with both legs straight in the air against a wall. Your buttocks should be touching, or nearly touching, the wall.

Action: Keep both knees fully extended and spread your legs as far apart as possible, sliding them along the wall to the sides. Maintain the stretch for 30 seconds. Return to the starting position and then repeat.

The stretch: Inner thighs of both legs.

Variations: Bend your ankles, and point your toes toward your face to increase the stretch behind the calves.

Spread one leg out to the side, but keep the other leg pointing toward the ceiling as in the starting position.

Keep one leg pointing toward the ceiling and bend the other so the foot comes close to the groin.

If you are very limber in the Backward Rolling exercise, Region III, spread your legs apart into a wide "V". From this position, continue into a backward roll until your toes touch the floor at the outer side of each shoulder. Your buttocks will no longer be in contact with the wall.

To return from this position, slowly bring your legs together, lower them to your chest, roll both knees to one side, and get up from a sidelying position.

Elevating the legs overhead is a part of the after-ski relaxation routine. Incorporate all or part of these variations in your relaxation. Keep your emphasis on slow, easy stretches for the Basic Program as well as for relaxation.

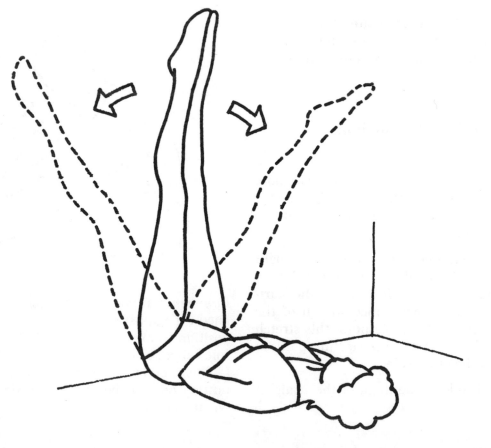

67. Combination Stretch (Most difficult)

Starting position: Lie on your side with your elbow bent underneath your body for support. Bend your bottom leg for balance.

Action: Raise your top leg as high as you possibly can and grasp your foot or ankle with your hand. Sit up slightly and pull your leg and your head close together. Keep your knee fully straightened. Hold this stretch for 15 seconds. Lower and repeat.

The stretch: Back of thigh, inner thigh.

Variation: Pull your foot toward your head to add more stretch to the calf.

Comments: This advanced variation is only for those who are very limber in the hamstring and adductor regions.

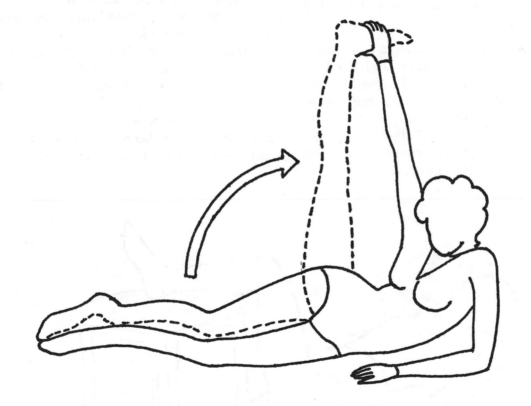

CATEGORY: STRENGTHENING

Special Instructions

Exercises in this region include both the isometric and isotonic types. Choose exercises from both for your Basic Program.

68. Horizontal Leg Swing

Starting position: Lie on your back with one leg straight on the floor and the other leg bent over the seat of a chair.

Action: Raise the straightened leg a few inches off the floor. Keep the kneecap and the toes pointing toward the ceiling at all times. Slowly swing the leg to the side and then return it to the starting position, but do not put your leg down between repetitions. Follow the guidelines for strengthening to determine the number of repetitions. Repeat for both legs.

Muscular work: Inner thigh, when leg swings inward; outer hip and thigh, when leg swings outward.

Comments: Keeping the stationary leg bent over the seat of a chair helps to give your pelvis more stability and prevents your body from falling over when your leg moves outward.

It is very important that your moving leg *not* roll outward when you swing it to the side. If it does, perhaps you are trying to swing it out further than you should. Your leg should move out only to a 45-degree angle. Always check to see that your toes and your kneecap are pointing upward, not outward.

If this exercise produces a strong strain on your lower back, discontinue it.

This exercise strengthens the inner thigh muscles when your leg moves inward, and the outer thigh muscles when your leg moves outward. In addition, keeping your knee fully extended strengthens the front of the thigh.

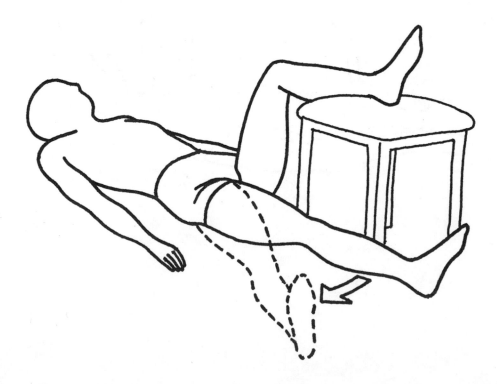

69. Sidelying Lower Leg Lift

Starting position: Lie on your side, with the uppermost foot on the edge of a padded chair and the lower leg directly underneath it. Keep both knees straight.

Action: Raise the lower leg to touch the underside of the chair. Hold it in this position for a moment before lowering it slowly to the starting position. Repeat.

Muscular work: Inner thigh of the lower leg and upper leg. (Isometric tension of the upper leg and isotonic tension of the lower leg.)

Progression: Add weight to the lower ankle, starting with small weights of one or two pounds.

Comments: This is an excellent exercise for strengthening the muscles of the inner thigh, which are rarely used in everyday activities. It is more difficult than exercise 68.

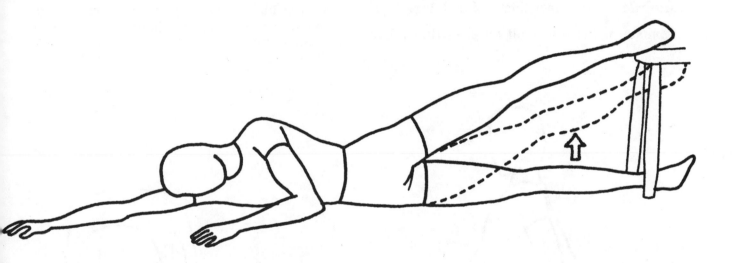

70. Chair Squeeze, Isometric

Starting position: Sit on the floor with your hands behind you for support, your knees straight, and your feet straddling the outside of a sturdy chair.

Action: Press both ankles simultaneously against the chair legs, trying to push the chair legs together. Maintain the squeezing action for at least 10 seconds. Slowly release the tension, relax and repeat.

Muscular work: Inner thighs of both legs.

Comments: Place a small towel or thin pillow between your ankles and the chair leg for comfort.

If you have suffered any previous strain or sprain to the ligaments on the inner side of your knee joint, do not do this exercise. You can, however, do a different type of adductor isometric by placing a pillow between bent knees and trying to flatten the pillow with your knee pressure. This second position gives work to the adductor muscles without causing stress over the knee joint itself.

The adductor exercise can be followed immediately by abductor exercises for the outer thigh using a similar chair straddling position. Refer to exercise 76.

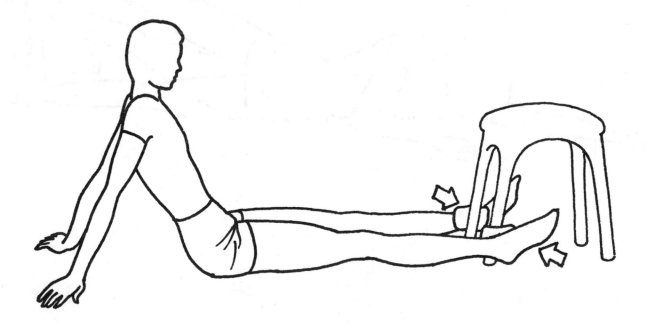

71. Partner Squeeze, Isometric

Starting position: Stand in front of a seated partner. Your legs are on the outside of your partner's knees, which are spread apart slightly. If one or both of you has little natural padding around the knees, use a towel in between your knees and his knees for comfort. Keep your knees slightly flexed.

Action: You begin the exercise by squeezing your partner's knees together. Your partner applies pressure outward, just enough to prevent you from actually moving his knees. *You* give the signal when to release tension. Hold the tension as long as you feel comfortable, at least 15 seconds. You tell your partner to ease off first. Alternate positions with your partner and repeat.

Muscular work: Inner thighs of your legs, outer hips and thighs of your partner's legs.

Comments: Do this exercise in combination with exercise 77.

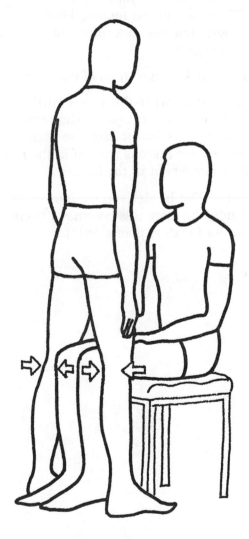

72. Sitting Thigh Squeeze, Isometric and Isotonic

Starting position: Sit on the edge of a chair with your feet flat on the floor, your hands crossed inside of the opposite knee, and your upper body leaning forward slightly.

Action: Squeeze your knees inward while you resist the motion with your hands, pushing outward. There should be tension built up in the inner thigh, but no movement of the knees. Relax and repeat.

Muscular Work: Inner thigh of each leg.

Variation: Start with the knees further apart and *move* them inward against the resistance of your hands. This is the isotonic form of the exercise because there is tension in the muscles as well as movement of the limbs.

Comments: The harder you push outward with your hands, the more this becomes a strengthening exercise for the upper chest, too.

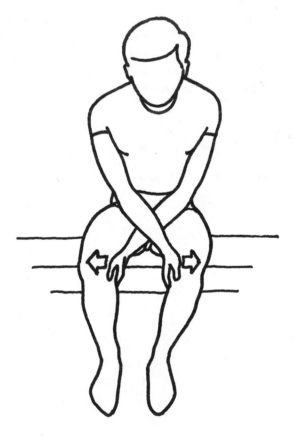

19 || Region VIII—Outer Hip (Hip Abduction)

ANATOMY

The muscles for abduction are located on the outer side of the pelvis, attaching from the pelvis to the outer side of the thigh bone.

Contraction of these muscles brings your leg from the center of your body to the side. It also works to stabilize your pelvis, keeping it level when you stand on one leg.

FUNCTION

Strong hip abduction is needed for the movements of stemming one or both skis out to the side, moving the uphill ski in a side-step, and providing a firm base of support for the twists and turns of the upper body in aggressive, advanced skiing. Pressing the skis out into a snowplow position and maintaining them while the rotator muscles turn the hips inward requires sustained abductor strength.

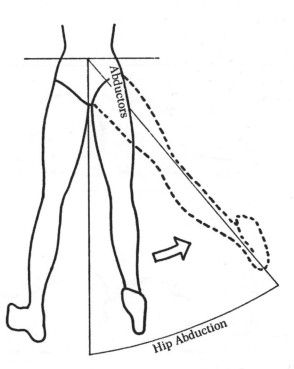

CATEGORY: STRETCHING

73. Sidelying Hip Stretch

Starting position: Lie on your side at the edge of a bed, with your bottom knee bent. You should be close enough to the edge to lower your top leg behind you.

Action: Lower the top leg over the edge, a combination of placing it behind and below your body. Let it hang in this position over the edge for 15 seconds. Return it to the starting position and repeat.

The stretch: Outer hip and thigh of the top leg.

Variation: If you don't feel much of a stretch, add a small weight of about two pounds to your ankle to increase the pull. Be sure that you stay on your side and do not simply roll backward with the added weight, giving the illusion that your leg is stretched lower.

Comment: The starting position, sidelying, is the same position used to begin the Sidelying Upper Leg Lift, 74, for abductor strengthening. Do these one after the other as long as your bed is firm enough to support you during exercise 74.

It is recommended that you repeat exercise 36, Counter-Rotated Body Twist. It provides a stretch to the hip of the bent knee if you roll your knee all the way over toward the floor. Remember to keep your shoulders flat on the floor.

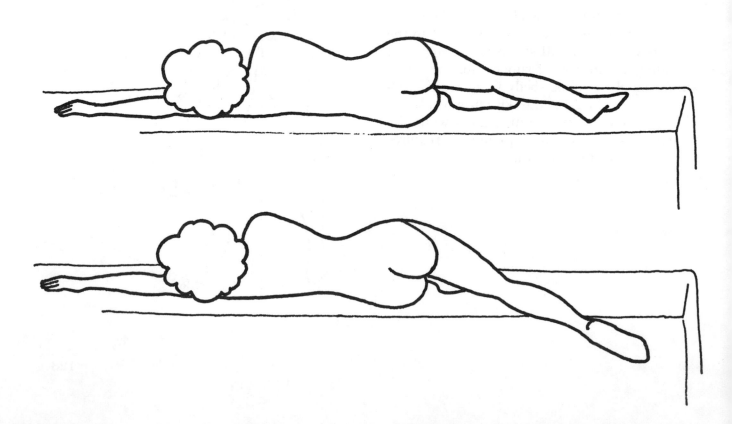

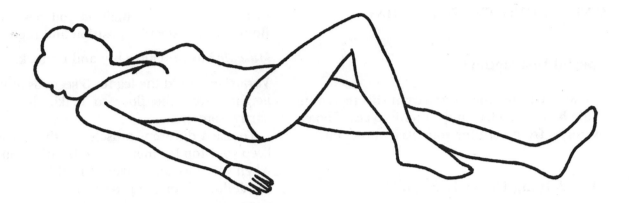

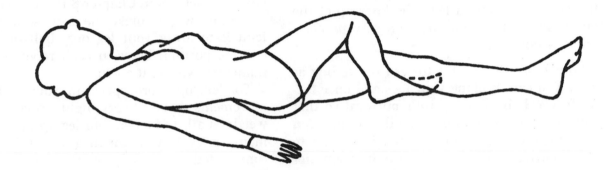

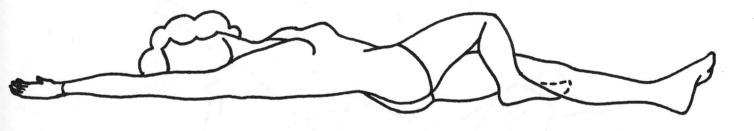

Counter-rotated body twist

CATEGORY: STRENGTHENING

Special Instructions

The strengthening exercises in this region include both isometric and isotonic types. Choose exercises from both for your Basic Program.

74. Sidelying Upper Leg Lift

Starting position: Lie on your side on the floor with the bottom knee bent for balance and the top knee fully extended. The top leg is *behind* the foot of the bottom leg. The kneecap of the top leg faces the same direction as your nose, that is, straight ahead.

Action: Raise the top leg toward the ceiling as far as you can, keeping your toes and knee facing forward. If your leg rolls outward so that your kneecap and toes point to the ceiling, you are doing the exercise incorrectly. The goal is to raise your leg in a pure, sideward direction, *not*

to raise your leg as high as you possibly can. Return to the starting position and repeat.

Muscular work: Outer hip and buttock.

Variations: Hold the leg for 5 seconds at various heights from the floor to make the exercise partly isometric.

To use a different muscle for the movement, keep your top leg more to the front of your body when you raise and lower it. In this position you can follow all of the progressions that are mentioned for the standard position.

Progression: To make the exercises more difficult, add weights to your ankle. Read the specific instructions in Chapter 8 for details.

Another way to make the exercise more difficult is to lower your leg only halfway to the starting position between each repetition, and immediately raise it again.

To develop more speed in your abduction movements, use a very light weight or no weight at all, and move your leg up and down as many times as you can in a 15- or 30-second time period.

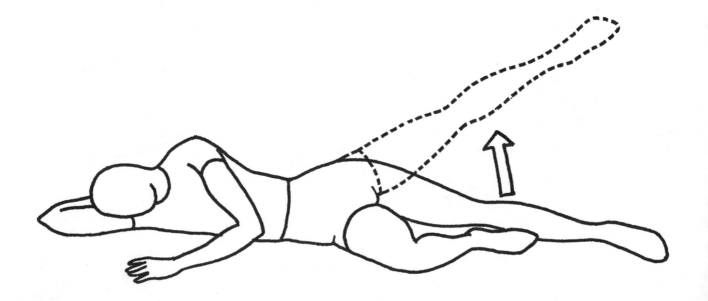

75. Side Leg Lift, Standing

Starting position: Stand sideways on a step, with one leg dangling over the edge. Hold onto the railing for balance.

Action: Raise the dangling leg out to the side, keeping your knee fully extended and your kneecap facing forward. Keep your upper body erect at all times. Repeat.

Muscular work: Outer side of hips. Isometric for the standing leg and isotonic for the moving leg.

Progression: Add weights to your ankle.

Comments: If you have to dip your body to the opposite side in order to raise the leg out, then you are using weights that are too heavy.

If you are dipping your body to the opposite side and you haven't used any additional weights, then you should substitute the back-lying Horizontal Leg Swing, exercise 68, until your abductor muscles are stronger.

If you can perform the standard standing movement ten or more times easily, but your leg doesn't go out very far, you may have good abductor strength combined with tightness of the adductors in the inner thigh. Work on adductor stretching exercises, Chapter 18, if this is your problem.

76. Chair Spread, Isometric

Starting position: Sit on the floor with both legs straight on the floor and both ankles inside the legs of a sturdy chair or stool. Place a towel between your ankles and the chair for comfort.

Action: Try to spread the chair legs apart. Hold the spreading tension for at least 15 seconds. Relax, then repeat.

Muscular work: Along the outer thigh and hip of both legs.

Variation: Sit in a bathtub with your legs straight on the bottom of the tub and with your feet touching the side walls. Press your feet outward into the walls as you did with the chair. Hold the position for at least 15 seconds.

Comments: A good combination of exercises is this exercise followed immediately with any of the seated adductor stretches, Chapter 18. Pressing outward isometrically with the abductors has an inhibiting effect on adductor tension, allowing the adductors to be stretched more easily.

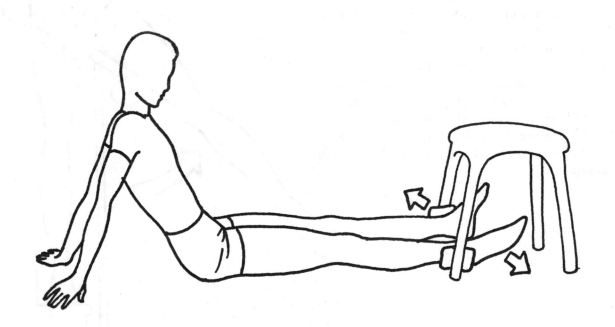

77. Partner Thigh Squeeze, Isometric

Starting position: Stand with your knees *inside* the knees of your seated partner, flexing your knees slightly for comfort.

Action: Press your legs outward while your partner presses inward.

Muscular work: Outer hips and thighs of your legs, inner thighs of your partner's legs.

Comments: For the safety and comfort of your partner, let *him* tell *you* when to cease the pressure, since the muscles of the inner thigh are weaker and more susceptible to muscle pulls if given an unexpected and strong stretch.

Do this exercise in combination with exercise 71 in the adductor region.

To do both the inner and outer thigh squeezes, you can maintain either the standing or the sitting position and just move your knees either to the inside or the outside of your partner's. It's a good idea for the partners to change positions so that one person isn't always standing and the other always sitting.

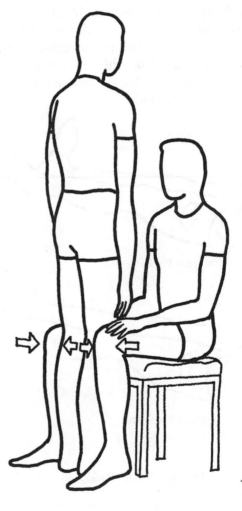

20 | Region IX—Hip Rotations (Internal Rotation and External Rotation)

ANATOMY

The contraction of many small muscles located deep within the pelvis, in combination with the strong contraction of the buttock muscles, produces the movements of external rotation. Muscles located on the outer side of the pelvis work to turn the leg for internal rotation, is a relatively weak motion.

External Rotation

Internal Rotation

Rotation of Hip, Backlying

FUNCTION

Strong rotators give you more strength to direct your skis inward and outward for all types of turns and for sustaining pressure on the ski edges.

Flexibility of the rotators for skiers comes into play for such activities as the herringbone climb, where the legs are turned outward, and the snowplow position, where the legs are turned inward.

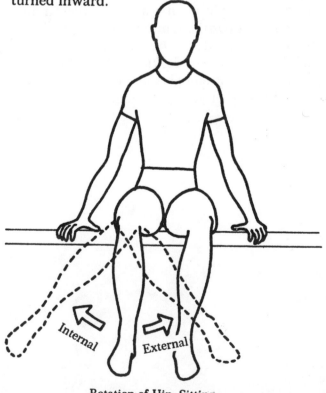

Rotation of Hip, Sitting

CATEGORY: STRETCHING

Stretches for the rotator muscles of the hips, both internal and external rotation, are best done in combination with other movements of the hips.

Refer to the following exercises, which include rotation:

For internal rotation:
   Counter-rotated Body Twist, 36
   Hip Rotation, Prone, 78
   Leg Cross Over, 79

For external rotation:
   Adductor Spread, Knees Bent, 64
   Hip Rotation, Prone, 78
   Leg Cross Over, 79

CATEGORY: STRENGTHENING

78. Hip Rotation, Prone (Internal and external rotation)

Starting position: Lie flat on your stomach with both legs bent at the knee, the shins perpendicular to the floor.

Action: Keep your thighs on the floor, knees close together, and separate your feet as far as possible. Each foot will move about halfway to the floor, making a 45-degree angle with the floor. Slowly return your legs to the starting position and let them cross over each other. Return them to the starting position. Relax and repeat.

Muscular work: Buttock, outer hip, and back of the thigh.

Progression: Add weights to your ankle. The additional weight should provide a slight stretch to your hip when your leg is at the extreme right or left. This is an exercise that can be started with your ski boot as the first weight.

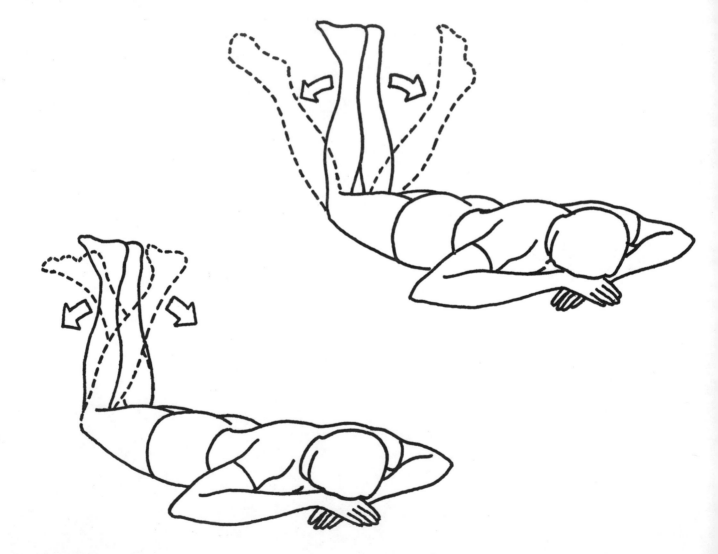

79. Leg Cross Over (Internal and external rotation)

Starting position: Lie on your back with both legs straight. Your arms are spread out to the sides for balance.

Action: Keep one leg as straight as possible and cross it over the other one, touching your big toe to the floor. Lift it back up and over to the other side, touching your little toe to the floor. Continue from side to side: big toe, little toe, big toe, little toe, etc., without resting your leg on the floor between each lift. Keep your shoulders flat on the floor at all times. Repeat for the other leg.

Follow the guidelines for Strengthening, Chapter 8, to determine the number of repetitions.

Muscular work: Inner thigh, outer thigh and buttock.

Progression: Add weights to your ankle and proceed as above.

Comments: The extreme positions of leg rotation to both sides give a stretch to the opposing muscles. For example, when the leg is rolled inward onto the big toe by action of the internal rotators, the external rotators are getting a stretch.

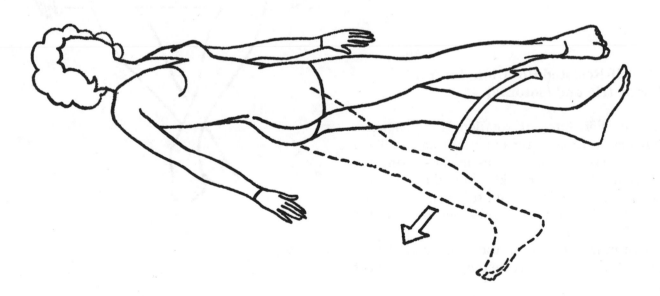

80. Self-Resisted Rotation, External (Isometric and isotonic)

Starting position: Sit in a comfortable, firm chair with your feet crossed at the ankles and your knees spread apart. Your feet should *not* touch the floor.

Action: For *external* rotation: Press your ankles into each other while keeping the knees apart. Tighten the muscles in your buttocks to increase this isometric tension.

Start with your knees close together and then spread them apart under tension to strengthen with movement.

Muscular work: Outer hips and thighs of both legs.

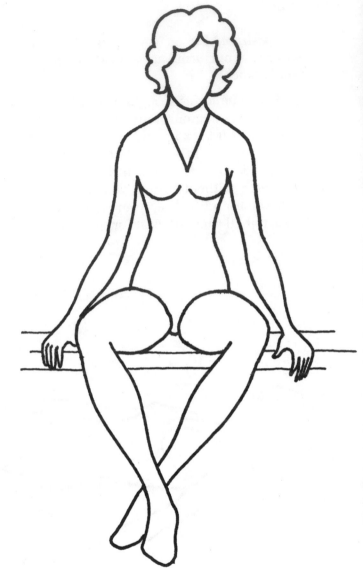

81. Self-Resisted Rotation, Internal (Isometric and isotonic)

Action: For *internal* rotation, use the same starting position as for external rotation. Then very slowly roll your knees inward, using the resistance from your ankles to build up tension and prevent the knees and thighs from moving quickly. This exercise allows movement and is therefore isotonic.

Continue to try to roll the knees inward after they are touching to create the isometric form of the exercise.

Muscular work: Inner thighs and outer thighs of both legs.

Comments: These are exercises that can be done throughout the day whenever you sit in a chair.

21 | Region X—Buttock (Hip Extension)

ANATOMY

The muscles for hip extension are located primarily in the buttocks and in the back of the thigh. The hamstring muscles, which flex the knee, also assist in extending the hip.

Contracting these muscles brings your thigh behind your body.

Lack of flexibility in the hip extensor muscles is usually not a problem; but many people who are exceptionally tense and anxious do develop buttock tension that is not unlike nervous tension in the back of the neck.

FUNCTION

For cross-country skiers, strong hip extension helps to get a fully straightened leg after a strong kick. For the downhill skier, hip extension is used standing on one ski, in skating steps, and in climbing stairs wearing ski boots.

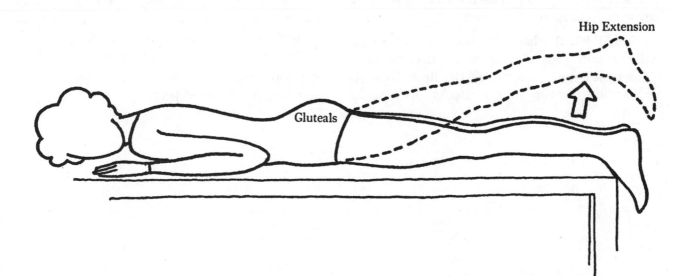

Gluteals

Hip Extension

CATEGORY: STRETCHING

Stretches for this region of the body are best done in combination with other movements, such as back extensor stretching and hamstring stretching.

CATEGORY: STRENGTHENING

Special Instructions

If you failed Physical Fitness test 5, start hip extension strengthening with exercises 82 and 83 (not illustrated). Later on, add 84.

82. Buttock Lift (Remedial)

Starting position: Lie on your back with your knees bent over two pillows. Let the pillows support your legs so you do not have to use your muscles to keep your legs bent.

Action: Push the backs of your knees into the pillows and your shoulders against the floor. This raises your buttocks off the floor. Hold for 5 seconds. Lower your buttocks. Release all

Refer to the following exercises which incorporate hip extensor stretching.

Total Body Roll, 35
Backward Roll Over, 37
Aerial Hamstring Stretch, 52

muscular tightness in the legs and buttocks before repeating.

Muscular work: Buttocks and back of thighs.

83. Buttock Squeeze, Isometric (Remedial)

Starting position: Lie on your stomach with a pillow underneath your abdomen and hips.

Action: Squeeze your buttocks together and hold the tension for 5 seconds. Release all of the tension in the muscles before repeating.

Muscular work: Buttocks.

Comments: Squeezing your buttocks together is a very good exercise to do at any time throughout the day, sitting or standing. An isometric buttock squeeze can be done inconspicuously without anyone knowing that you're exercising.

All you need to do is hold the tension for 5 seconds, relax, and repeat.

84. Single Leg Lift, Prone (Remedial)

Starting position: Lie on your stomach with a pillow underneath your abdomen and hips so that your head and feet are lower than your buttocks.

Action: Keep your legs straight and raise one leg in the air as high as you can, but not so high that your pelvis lifts off the pillow. Keep your leg in the air for a moment, then slowly lower it to the starting position. Repeat.

Muscular work: Buttock of the raised leg.

Variation: Refer to Chapter 15, Region IV, for the combined exercise, Alternate Arm and/or Leg Lift, 39.

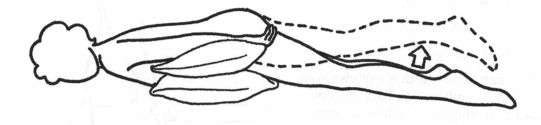

85. Bent Knee Leg Raise, Prone

Starting position: Lie on your stomach with a pillow underneath your abdomen and hips so that your head and feet are lower than your buttocks. Flex one knee so that your shin is perpendicular to the floor, your foot pointing toward the ceiling.

Action: Keep your leg in the bent position and lift it toward the ceiling until your thigh and knee come off the floor. Hold your leg in the air for a moment before lowering to the starting position. Keep the front of your pelvis on the pillow at all times. Repeat.

Comment: If you allow your pelvis to rise off the pillow in this exercise (or in the Single Leg Lift, Prone), you are using the mobility of your lower back to make it appear that your leg can go higher. Remember that the goal of this exercise is to use the hip extensor muscles, not to see how high you can raise your leg.

This exercise emphasizes the gluteal muscles more than the hamstrings in producing hip extension.

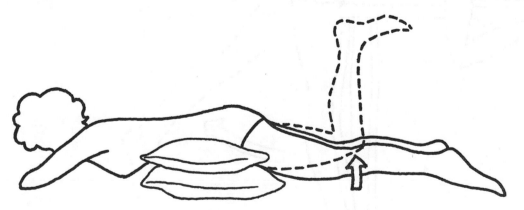

86. Rear Leg Lift, Standing

Starting position: Stand with your feet together, facing a countertop or railing for hand support.

Action: Keep both legs straight, knees fully extended, and raise one leg straight behind you. Keep your upper body erect at all times. Hold your leg in the air for a moment before slowly lowering it to the starting position.

Muscular work: Buttock of the raised leg.

Progression: Add weight to the ankle.

Variation: You can combine this exercise with the Side Leg Lift, Standing, 75. Face the counter to do both rear and side leg lifts. Alternate rear and side for each leg.

Instead of using the standard position standing upright, lean over a table so that your upper body is completely flat on the table. Grasp the sides of the tabletop with your hands. Start with both legs straight, as before, and lift one leg at a time behind you. Notice that in this position, your pelvis and low back are at a different angle and you will be able to raise your leg higher than in the standard position.

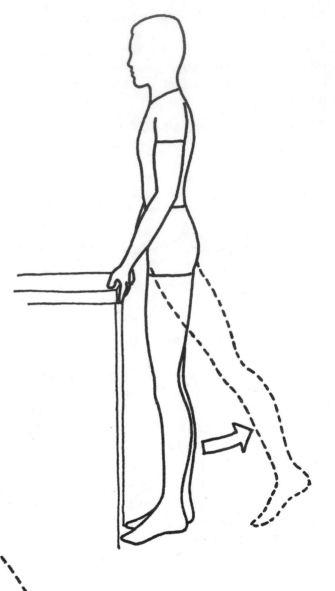

Variation

87. Scissors Kicking (Most difficult)

Starting position: Lie on your side with both legs straight.

Action: Keep your legs parallel to each other and alternately swing one leg forward while the other leg swings backward. Practice this slowly at first and gradually build up more speed. Do half of your repetitions on the right side and half on the left side.

Muscular work: Front, back, inner, and outer sides of hips and thighs of both legs.

Comments: This exercise combines hip flexion, hip extension, hip abduction, and hip adduction all in one exercise.

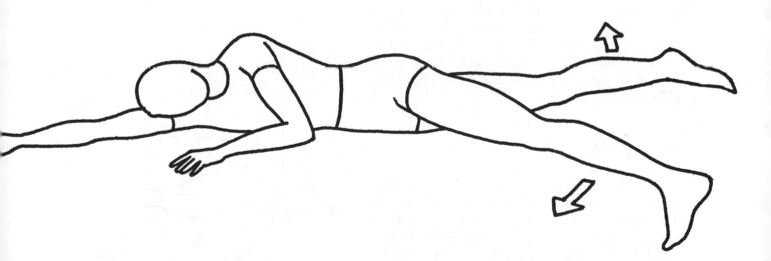

22 | Region XI—Calf and Ankle (Plantar Flexion)

ANATOMY

The calf muscles (gastrocnemius and soleus) originate behind and just below the knee joint, and insert into the back of the heel bone as one broad tendon, (Achilles tendon). The motion produced by contracting these muscles points the foot downward and is called plantar flexion. Contraction of these muscles also allows you to stand on your toes.

Good strength in the calf gives the cross-country skier a strong push-off.

Movement of the foot toward the shin is called dorsiflexion. Skiers who lean backward excessively are contracting the muscles of the lower leg along the shin, bringing the foot toward dorsiflexion. This causes the toes to come up into contact with the upper inside of the boot. If your shins ache after skiing, excessive use of these dorsiflexions may be the cause.

FUNCTION

Flexibility of the ankle that brings your toes toward your lower leg places the calf on stretch. The stretch is important for skiers who press their knees forward over the front of their boots. Good flexibility reduces the risk of serious injury if you catch a ski tip in the snow.

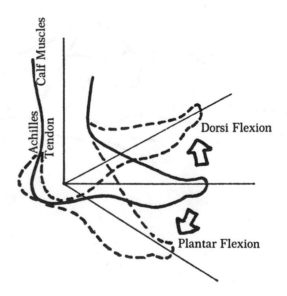

CATEGORY: STRETCHING

Special Instructions

If you failed Physical Fitness Quiz test 9, your Basic Program must include the calf stretching exercise Calf Stretch, Toward a Wall, 88.

88. Calf Stretch, Toward a Wall (Remedial)

Starting position: Stand arm's distance from a wall, facing it. Spread your feet apart so that one foot is ahead of the other, both feet pointing toward the wall. Place both forearms on the wall and rest your head on your hands.

Action: Let your front knee bend toward the wall but keep the back leg straight, with the foot flat on the floor. Continue to press the front knee forward until you feel a pulling sensation in the rear calf. It is crucial that the sole of the rear foot not come off the floor. Hold this stretch for 15 seconds. Maintain the same position, but allow the rear knee to bend slightly. This provides more stretch to a lower part of the calf than the first position. Hold this stretch for 15 seconds. Repeat.

The stretch: Upper and lower calves.

Variation: The same exercise can be done with both feet at the same time. Start with both feet parallel, legs close together when you lean on the wall.

Comment: If you feel no stretch in your calves, it is possible that you are not far enough from the wall.

89. Calf Stretch, Standing

Starting position: Stand on a step, with only the ball of your foot on the step and your heels hanging over the edge. Hold on to a rail for balance if needed.

Action: Keep your knees extended and lower your heels further below the step to feel a pull in the back of your calves and ankles. Hold the stretch for 15 seconds. Don't bounce. Relax, then repeat.

The stretch: Upper and lower calves.

Progression: Stretch one leg at a time by keeping the other foot off the step.

Stretch one or both calves without holding on to a rail to stimulate your balancing abilities.

Variation: Follow the same procedure, but keep your knees slightly flexed throughout the stretch instead of fully extended. You will feel the stretching feeling in the lower part of your calf.

Comment: By placing the ball of your foot on the edge of a step or on a curb, you can stretch the calf at various times throughout the day. This is especially helpful whenever you have been on your feet for a long time and are developing leg fatigue.

People who wear high-heeled shoes should be certain to give this region lots of stretching. The position of the foot when wearing these shoes places the calf muscles in a very shortened, contracted position.

It is recommended that you refer to the hamstring stretching exercises, Region VI. Many of these also provide a stretch for the calf muscles if they are particularly tight.

Some of these are:
Standing Floor Touch, 38
Single Leg Hamstring Stretch, 53
Special Remedial Hamstring Stretch, 54

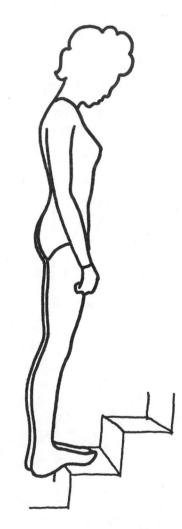

CATEGORY: STRENGTHENING

90. Toe Stands

Starting position: Stand with your toes on a step and your heels hanging lower, over the edge. Use a rail for hand support if needed.

Action: Rise up as high as possible onto your toes. Hold this position for a moment before lowering to the starting position. Repeat.

Muscular work: Upper and lower calves.

Progression: Perform the toe stands without any hand support.

    Perform the toe stand one leg at a time.

    Hold weights in your hands and perform as in the standard position with the added resistance.

Variation: If you have no step available, do the same exercise starting from the flatfooted position on the floor.

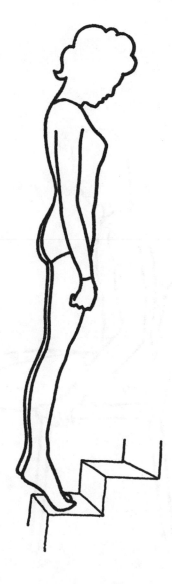

91. Partner Foot Push

Starting position: Sit with one leg extended at a level that is easily reached by your partner. For example, you may sit on a chair with your foot on a hassock while your partner sits on the floor in front of your foot.

Action: Start with your toes pointing toward the ceiling, then point your toes and foot toward your partner. Your partner should have his hands placed on the bottom of your foot to make it difficult for you to push your foot towards him. Once your foot is pointed all the way down, he should try to lift it up again, but you offer resistance. Hold this position for about 5 seconds. Relax and repeat with each foot.

Muscular work: Calf and toes.

Variation: Place a small pillow underneath your knee so you are doing the same foot push with the knee flexed instead of extended.

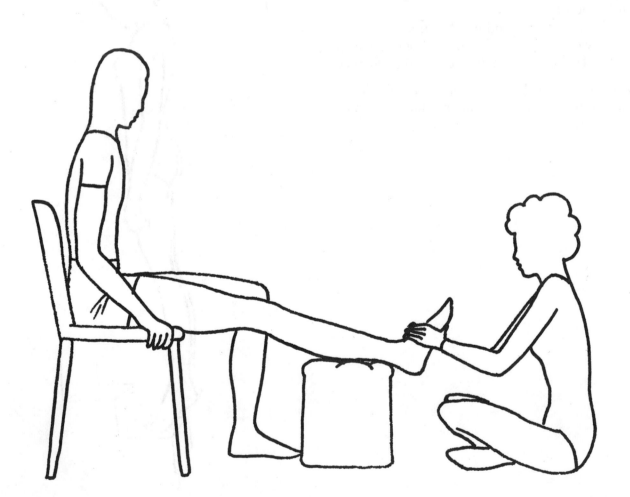

Continue in the same manner for the following directions of movement. For these you can keep your knee fully extended. Point your toes up to the ceiling and maintain the position for 5 seconds against your partner's hand resistance. Turn your foot inward and outward and hold each position for 5 seconds against your partner's resistance. Repeat the series of 4 directions with the other foot. Repeat the entire series 3 times.

Comment: The last set of exercises, combining foot movements in four directions, uses muscles located along the front and outer sides of the lower leg and ankle.

This technique of hand resistance can be used in the rehabilitation of foot, ankle, or knee injuries to develop strength and increased circulation in the muscles around these joints.

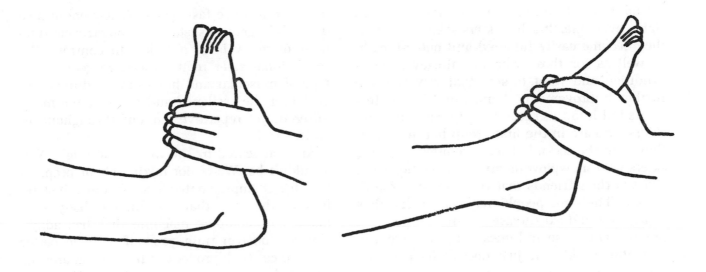

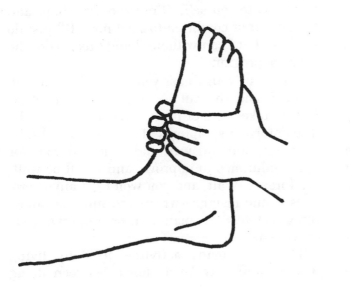

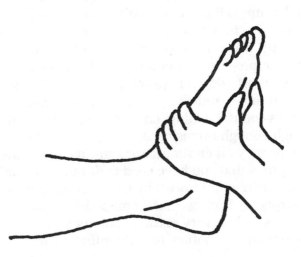

23 || Endurance Training Principles

Endurance training is for everyone. That's right, everyone. It's for skiers who know that they become easily fatigued and out-of-breath, as well as for those who are already in good condition and want to stay that way or make further improvements. Unfortunately, too few skiers fall into this second group; and there are skiers who are in the first group but think that they're in the second. These are often the same skiers who snowplow on an advanced slope and boast to their friends that they ski on "expert" terrain. The same people may believe that they can go out and ski themselves into shape. This practice is unwise and unsafe. For the average, recreational skier, it just doesn't happen that way.

You consider yourself to be an active person; otherwise you wouldn't be skiing or planning to take up skiing. But don't fool yourself into thinking that if you have a few ski outings a month this serves well as a training or maintenance program for endurance. It does not. Skiing itself doesn't provide a boost to your endurance unless you're doing continuous cross-country skiing on a frequent basis at a high enough intensity. Although skiing does not improve your endurance or stamina, good skiing requires that you have good endurance, not only muscular endurance but cardio-respiratory endurance. Professional, competitive downhill skiers utilize very static positions with a great economy of motion to streamline their movements to achieve fast speeds. Their endurance depends largely on sustained, isometric contractions of many large muscles. In contrast, the recreational skier requires a more generalized type of muscular and heart-lung endurance to give him the resilence and stamina for many different yet repetitive motions throughout an entire ski day.

Are you scared by the word "training"? You shouldn't be. We're not talking about preparation for Olympic contenders. Training just refers to the fact that the human body is a marvelous, complex machine that has adaptability. You can train yourself to have better endurance. With proper conditioning at any age your body can become more efficient. You need never say to yourself, "I'm too out of shape and too far out of condition to start now. I'll just do the best that I can without doing this part of the exercise program."

If you cut your finger you can wait for a scab to form and the cut to heal over completely. Nature takes care of itself. Give it time and the discomforting symptoms of a cold will subside. However, you can wait and wait and wait for your endurance to improve, and you'll be waiting forever. Wait, and you won't get anywhere. This is one instance where you must do something actively to maintain or improve your condition.

There are many activities in daily living where there may be a choice between doing something yourself or having someone else do it for you. You can mow your lawn, or pay someone else to mow it. You can give yourself a manicure, or pay a manicurist to do it for you. But when it comes to physical exercise, there is nothing that another person can do to you to improve your **endurance**. Your body is a machine which is energized through your own physical efforts.

As a type of machine, your body must have a fuel supply to produce energy for the work that it does. Oxygen is extremely important as a source of fuel for your working muscles. How the body uses oxygen determines in part how efficiently the body functions. The body's ability to use oxygen for everyday activities might be adequate, but for the extraordinary demands of some physical activities its utilization may be less than adequate. An unusually high demand can be put on you to ski long, continuous runs without stopping or to carry boots, skis, and poles uphill from the parking lot to the base lodge. How far you can go before getting out of breath tells you something about your body's ability to provide and use enough oxygen for the tasks you are doing.

The endurance part of ski conditioning is a matter of supply and demand. Either your body can keep itself energized for the activity you are doing or it can't. When your stamina is low you become easily tired and have to cease what you're doing due to fatigue. If your usual level of activity consists mostly of sitting in chairs interspersed with infrequent standing, walking, or riding in your car, you can't go out to ski for a few hours once in a while and expect your body to keep up with your ambition and motivation to ski well. Your desire to be an active sports participant and your desire to do well aren't going to be enough to see you through.

Endurance training means providing your heart and lungs with a healthy stress that causes them to work harder than usual. With proper conditioning your body adapts to this stress and you are then able to perform the same amount of work more easily. This stimulus of stress is called an "overload." It must be present in order for your endurance to improve. If improvement is your goal, endurance workouts which do not give you this stress are a waste of your time. The overload is a level of exercise which is enough to condition your cardio-respiratory system without being overly strenuous.

The "fit" person delivers more energy to his muscles with less effort. With proper training, there is less strain on the heart, lungs, and general circulation of the body. But only certain kinds of exercise promote this kind of fitness. Only exercise that stimulates the continuous flow of blood through the heart and large skeletal muscles will help cardio-respiratory fitness. Exercises such as weight lifting and isometrics, which strengthen skeletal muscles by shortening them, inhibit the blood flow and therefore the oxygen supply. Activities such as diving or bowling are too brief to promote cardio-respiratory fitness.

The "fit" person has a lower pulse rate, a higher cardiac output volume of blood pumped out with each beat, and a better intake and regulation of oxygen than the less fit person. Pulse rates raised during physical exercise return more quickly to normal in the fit person. With cardio-respiratory training the heart muscle itself becomes stronger, pumps more efficiently, and the rate is lowered. Why is a slower heart rate better? A slow rate allows more time for the heart to fill with incoming blood so that when it does pump blood out, more blood is pumped out with each beat.

The type of exercise you need to achieve this type of fitness is an exercise activity that is rhythmic and repetitive, using many large skeletal muscles. Jogging, running, rowing, cycling, swimming, jumping rope, ice or roller skating, even vacuuming and some types of dancing can form the basis for an endurance workout. These activities must be done long enough to provide the stress that will help train your body. What all of these activities have in common is that they are isotonic (dynamic) rather than isometric (static). In addition, they can be performed continuously at a level of intensity that is high enough to provide the necessary overload. Contrast these activities with doubles tennis or volleyball, which don't provide enough continuous, dynamic work to be suitable for endurance training.

Of course, many of the exercises that do not promote cardio-respiratory fitness have other benefits for building strength, skill, or other characteristics. A certain type of exercise isn't intrinsically good or bad. It just depends on whether it suits your purposes. It matters whether you want to develop only strength, such as the weight lifter or body builder, or whether you want good strength and good endurance at the same time. It matters whether your goal is to be a competitive or a recreational downhill skier.

The kind of continuous, sustained exercise we're talking about is called "aerobic" exercise. Literally, aerobic means "with oxygen." This type of exercise requires a steady supply of oxygen to the exercising muscles. When we talk about overloading the cardio-respiratory system we're talking about overloading and improving the body's oxygen transport system. Cross-country and, to a lesser extent, downhill skiing require that the skier have good aerobic capacity.

Aerobic capacity is often used as a measure of physical fitness. It refers to the maximum volume of oxygen that the body can utilize in an all-out physical effort. Even though you don't ski or train yourself to the point of exhaustion, you can still learn a lot about endurance fitness and how to achieve it by knowing some things about aerobics. Your aerobic capacity increases with proper physical conditioning and decreases with deconditioning.

Most people who faithfully follow a training program will show an increase in their maximum oxygen uptake. For skiing this means that the more oxygen your body can take in and utilize, the better your stamina. It means longer ski runs with less fatigue. Studies done on the muscular composition of competitive downhill and cross-country skiers, long distance runners, and cyclists showed that they have more of the type of muscle fiber best suited for endurance work. Their skeletal muscles have more of the aerobic type of fiber than weight lifters and sprinters, whose muscular composition is better suited for the type of physical activity requiring less of a continuous oxygen supply. The type of muscle fiber that a person possesses is purely genetic and cannot be changed. However, endurance training can improve your capacity no matter what your inherent muscular constitution may be.

With training, more oxygen is not only transported *to* the muscle region, but more oxygen can be extracted *from* the blood to be used by the muscle tissue. The blood not only has to get the oxygen to the parts of the body that need it, but it must also be carrying enough oxygen to meet the demand and be able to give it up to the muscles. When you exercise at a level suitable enough to improve your cardio-respiratory fitness, you are producing a "training effect" by enhancing the function of many very important links in the heart-lung-circulation-muscle network.

Achieving a training effect is the ultimate goal of your endurance fitness program. As with other parts of your physical fitness program for strength and flexibility, this too is individualized. How you actually go about doing this may be very different from the way a friend of yours does it, even though you may both be the same age and ski with the same level of proficiency.

The maximal aerobic capacity of the body is the point at which the heart and circulatory system are delivering as much oxygen as they possible can to the body tissues. The lungs may be bringing oxygen to the bloodstream, but the body cannot transport it any faster. Therefore, one of the most important parts of your endurance exercising is to be able to determine what level of exercising you need to enhance this system.

There are many different ideas about how one should develop cardio-respiratory fitness. There are those at one extreme who believe that each athlete has to determine for himself the kind of fatigue and energy expenditure that enables him to improve his endurance without relying on any specific measurements. This is pretty much a "do what feels right" approach. At the other extreme are the laboratories where very elaborate and sophisticated instrumentation is used to furnish detailed and highly accurate data about heart and lung functions at rest, during, and after exercise. This type of evaluation isn't available or practical for everyone, especially for those who take regular and frequent exercise sessions. When available, it certainly is extremely helpful.

In general, during exercise your body requires:

1. Increased total body oxygen consumption.
2. Increased pulmonary (lung) ventilation.
3. Increased cardiac output.
4. Increased oxygen extracted by the muscle tissue.

The general effects of endurance training are:

1. Increased efficiency of the respiratory system to take in more oxygen with each breath and pass it from the lungs into the bloodstream.

2. To increase the efficiency of the cardiac system by improving the strength of the heart muscle, the strength of the pumping mechanism, and the general blood circulation.

Most exercise physiologists agree that cardio-respiratory capacity is enhanced when you sustain your dynamic, physical activity for 20 to 30 minutes several times a week in a safe range of intensity called the "target zone." The target zone is the intensity of exercise that makes an individual use 70 to 85 percent of his maximal aerobic capacity. In the laboratory, sophisticated scientific studies have shown that the maximum aerobic capacity is limited by the ability of the heart and the circulatory system to transport oxygen throughout the body.

For the average person there is no way to determine how much oxygen is being used during exercise; however, maximum aerobic capacity and the maximum heart rate of an individual are very close. Since the heart rate can be easily measured by anyone who knows how to take his own pulse, the heart rate can serve as a personal guide for assessing this aspect of the training program.

The maximum heart rate (MHR) of an individual, man or woman, is roughly 220 minus the age. For a 30-year-old this would be 220−30, or 190 beats per minute. For a 55-year-old the MHR is 220−55, or 165 beats per minute.

For the 30-year-old to use 70 to 85 percent of his MHR, his target zone exercising puts his pulse rate in the range of 136 to 165 beats per minute; whereas for the 55-year-old the range is 115 to 140 beats per minute.

Remember that this formula is an estimate that is accurate for most people. You may have heart rate values slightly higher or lower than the formula predicts and still be achieving a cardio-respiratory effect because of individual differences. Always check with your personal doctor if you have any doubts or questions about appropriate exercise for your physical condition.

Before you begin to exercise, take your pulse rate while resting. Then begin the warm-up part of your training and take your pulse after 10 minutes. At this point your pulse should be less than 50 percent of the MHR for your age level.

The stimulus part of your training comes next. This is when you are exercising with your pulse rate in your target zone.

Take your pulse after 3 minutes, 10 minutes, and thereafter at 5-minute intervals throughout the remainder of the stimulus until you are more familiar with the level of effort you need to be in your target zone. Use Chart A to record these values. Chart B shows a sample exercise pattern for an individual 40 years of age. If the pulse rate is below your target zone, exercise more intensely. If it is above your target zone, be less vigorous.

After the stimulus period there is a 5- to 10-minute cool-down period. During this time, lessen the intensity of your exercise but do not stop it completely. Stopping suddenly leaves blood pooled in the muscular areas that were working very hard during the exercise activity. Take your pulse at 5 and 10 minutes into the cool-down to determine if your heart rate has returned to normal within this time.

Your heart rate should be at 120 beats per minute or less after 5 minutes of rest and below 100 beats per minute after 10 minutes of rest. After a while you will become more familiar with the feelings you get when exercising in your target zone. You won't have to take your pulse rate each time to know that you are exercising properly.

With endurance training, you must re-evaluate your status from time to time to determine whether the same amount of exercise is still enough to put you into the target zone and produce a training effect. After 2 to 3 weeks most people start to improve their performance. After 4 to 6 weeks there are usually noticeable changes if you have been regular in your exercising. You will be able to exercise more easily, begin to sleep better, and be less tired at the end of a day.

To make further progress as your body becomes more trained you must exercise with more vigor. If you have been walking briskly to get into your target zone, start jogging for part of the time. Increase the brake resistance on your bicycle if you have been cycling. Swim more laps in the pool or increase the number of skips per minute with your jump rope. Re-evaluate yourself every 4 to 6 weeks. When you are developing your own program, remember to begin exercising at the lower range of your target zone and to progress by emphasizing a longer duration of exercise, rather than a greater intensity of exercise, during the first few months. This means that you should increase the amount of time that you exercise at the lower intensity in each session before pushing yourself to exercise at the higher end of the target zone.

As with other aspects of physical fitness, endurance is individual. However, there is one common denominator: getting interested and staying interested in endurance activities (if you aren't already) will be easier and healthier if your body is comfortable doing repetitive work. You have to be able to keep jogging or jumping rope, bicycle riding or rowing long enough to make it an endurance activity.

Too often people start an endurance program with very good intentions, but then give it up. Why? One of the main reasons is that they develop muscle and joint pains and discontinue due to discomfort. Some people believe that this is just a necessary part of starting a new exercise routine.

It doesn't have to be that way. There's no reason that you should have to become physically hurt and easily discouraged. Also, once you are motivated to start an exercise program, the quickest way to lose your enthusiasm is to attempt to do too much too soon. Too often people make the mistake of trying to make up for lost time by overdoing it in the beginning. In the majority of cases, this approach is doomed to fail.

CHART A

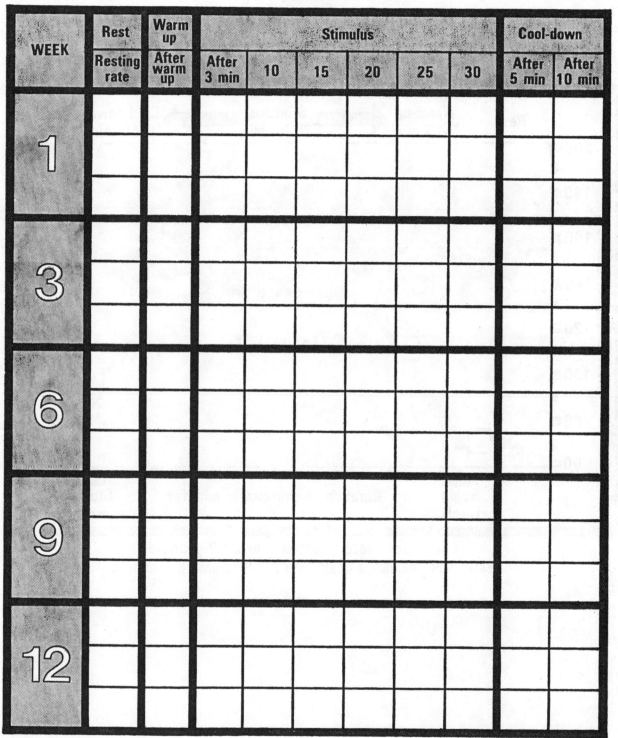

| WEEK | Rest | Warm up | Stimulus | | | | | | Cool-down | |
	Resting rate	After warm up	After 3 min	10	15	20	25	30	After 5 min	After 10 min
1										
3										
6										
9										
12										

CHART B

ENDURANCE EXERCISE TRAINING

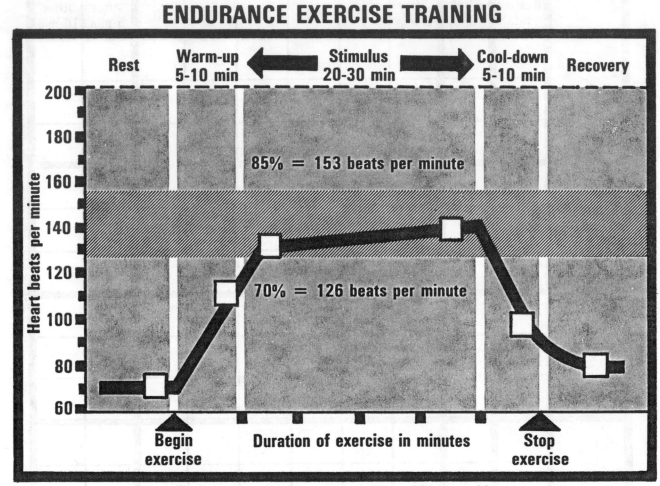

Rest | Warm-up 5-10 min | ← Stimulus 20-30 min → | Cool-down 5-10 min | Recovery

85% = 153 beats per minute

70% = 126 beats per minute

Heart beats per minute

Begin exercise   Duration of exercise in minutes   Stop exercise

Endurance exercise pattern for a 40-year-old
Estimated maximum heart rate is 180 beats per minute

What should you do to reduce the likelihood of these things happening to you? Make sure before you start any endurance exercising that you are already doing daily stretching exercises. When you begin endurance sessions, again make sure that you do specific stretches at the start of each session. Once you begin to feel limber and more comfortable doing regular stretching you'll feel that you want to do more active exercises. You'll have a greater interest and physical tolerance for endurance training.

Endurance training must be done regularly. Doing it once in a while is *not* better than not doing it at all. You're not being fair to yourself if you try to put your body through the mild to vigorous rigors of endurance work on an occasional basis. It must also be regular if you want to maintain your improvements. It's like dieting. You can't go on a reducing diet and achieve your desired weight, then return to excessive eating and hope to maintain your weight loss.

Any activity is suitable as long as it gets you into your target zone for at least 20 minutes. Once you develop endurance at one particular activity, you must remember that this does not necessarily carry over to other endurance-type activities. You may have developed endurance for 20 minutes of bicycle riding, but if you switch after 6 weeks to jumping rope you may find that your endurance for the jumping is not comparable to what it was while cycling. The body is using different muscles in different ways and it takes time for it to adapt and become as efficient at the new patterns of movement as at the previous ones.

If you are bicycle riding, make sure that your seat and handle bars are adjusted properly. With your toe on the pedal at its lowest point there should be only a very slight bend at the knee. If the seat is too high or too low, your leg muscles won't work as efficiently as they should. When your hands are on the handlebars your trunk should be relaxed and inclined for-

ward slightly. Squirming to keep yourself perched on the bicycle seat should not be a part of the exercise. The resistance setting on your bicycle should be gauged so that you can reproduce the same setting day to day. Remember that your heart rate is your guideline, not the resistance setting of the bike. Electric bicycles? Forget them.

When cycling out-of-doors, you can develop a training program by choosing a route that gives you about 5 minutes of flat cycling for a warm-up, followed by 20 minutes of uphill riding, and finishes with flat riding for cooling down. Check your pulse during the stimulus period to make sure that you are exercising in your target zone.

When swimming, use the same stroke throughout your training sessions. This allows your muscular system to adapt more readily and efficiently to the work. Changing from stroke to stroke makes it more difficult for your body to maintain improvements when it is always having to "relearn."

Swim continuously but easily for the first 5 minutes as a warm-up. Go faster for the next 5 to 10 minutes, taking your pulse to check if you are in the target zone. If you are, resume your pace for at least 20 minutes total stimulus period in the target zone. Stay in the water for 5 to 10 minutes afterward to cool down.

Jumping rope is an excellent way to develop agility, rhythm, timing and cardio-respiratory endurance. Jumping places a lot of stress on the knee and ankle joints; so practice on a carpet or other padded surface and wear comfortable, thick rubber-soled shoes. It's advisable to loosen the neck, shoulder, and back muscles with stretching before each jumping session. Pay special attention to the lower leg and feet by doing calf stretches and movements of the ankles and toes in all directions before starting.

For the warm-up, begin without the rope and loosen up all over with some easy hopping in place or around the room, using any combina-

You can increase your agility and speed by doing another type of hopping exercise without a rope. Try hopping in a low position without fully extending your legs. Hop with both feet together from side to side over a small book, over a stack of telephone books and progress to hops over a small bench.

Hop several times on each foot and then switch to the other foot. You can do combinations of 8 hops on the right, 8 on the left, 6 on the right, then 6 on the left, 4 on the right, and so on.

With feet together, hop quickly on and off a step; start with one foot already on the step and

tions of one and two-footed bounces. Start with 15-second intervals with rests in between and gradually work up to 2 minutes of continuous, comfortable bouncing. When you can do this easily for at least 100 repetitions, practice with the rope, starting with 50 jumps. Increase by adding 10 more jumps per day. Use your heart rate as your guide. Jumping faster and faster is not a necessary goal. Experiment with walking and alternate jumping to sustain your activity for the full stimulus period. For jumping rope, use the point of breathlessness as the end of your stimulus period.

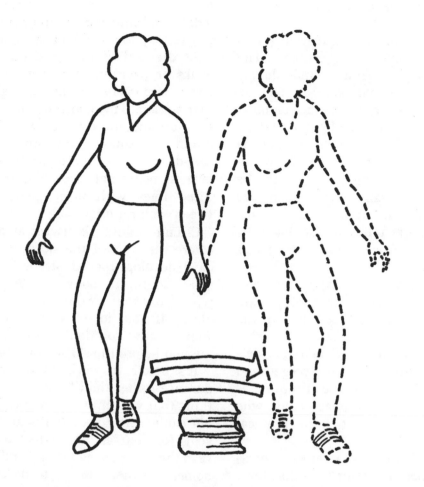

as you use that leg to boost you up to it, switch your feet in the air so that your opposite foot lands on the step. It's like a "scissors" movement in the air. Alternate starting with the right and left feet. Try steps of different heights.

Advance all of these hopping exercises by increasing the height of the step or bench that you are using and by increasing the number of repetitions. To use these exercises for endurance training, check your pulse rate after a few minutes of vigorous work and then modify your pace as needed. If your pulse rate should be higher for you to derive more benefit, then try to hop faster. If you are working at a range that is a little too high, then modify by exercising more slowly.

Tom Reynolds, director of skiing programs at the University of Maine at Farmington, suggests a slalom technique with a jump rope. To do this, you keep your feet 3 to 6 inches apart, knees slightly bent, and move your knees from side to side to simulate quick edge changing. In his program for ski racers he also recommends a "folding chair jump" which is done with two turns of the rope for every time that your knees are raised up very high toward your chest. This is similar to the way the knees are pushed up under the body by a bump while skiing. It is also a very demanding exercise, not suitable for everyone.

For your general jump rope program try to vary the type of footwork and leg patterns. The variety of steps to choose from include double foot bounces, alternate foot bounces, feet together, feet spread apart, and heel-toe combinations. In many ways, skiing is a lot like that. At some time during an average ski day you may be using some or all of these leg actions. There are times when you are moving both legs in the same direction at the same time. There are other times when you are applying more force with one leg than the other or moving your weight further to the front, middle, or rear of your skis.

"Circuit" training is another type of exercise routine, but rather than being aerobic, it is anaerobic (without oxygen). It doesn't have the prolonged, sustained characteristics of aerobic work. Anaerobic activities rely on the body's short supply of readily available glycogen and other energy substances. This type of training is advisable only for the young and aggressive who ski "bump" runs with all-out, hard, physical effort.

Circuit training consists of a series of exercises, each performed one after the other for a short period of time, without a rest period in between. It's an excellent way for a group of young skiers to work together for intense bouts of exercise.

Each person starts out at a designated "station" in the room specified for a particular exercise movement. The exercises should be such activities as sit-ups, push-ups, jumping jacks, jumping rope, squat-thrusts, etc. Try to arrange the stations so that all of the lower body exercises aren't all on the same side of the room. To start the circuit each person takes a different station and does his exercise for the designated length of time. Try to do as many repetitions of the movement as you can within the time allotted. Time limits start with only 15 seconds and progress up to 45 seconds at each station.

At the end of the time limit, each person walks or jogs over to the next station in the circuit and everyone starts doing the exercise at that station. This continues until everyone has been around the circuit once. As with all endurance routines, always stretch before and do cool-down exercises afterward. Circuit training is most beneficial when it is repeated two or three times, with an adequate rest period between each round.

Circuit training is useful as a final tune-up before the start of the skiing season after you have developed good strength and flexibility throughout your body. It's better to skip this type of workout if your body isn't ready to handle it. If you do it too soon you'll only hurt yourself, and you don't want to be out of commission before the ski season begins.

It's better to work on other forms of endurance rather than force yourself to do something that you think you ought to be able to do, but can't. Know your limits and set reasonable goals for yourself. Don't feel that you have to rush through your flexibility and strength development so that you get to do circuit training. Circuit training is not for everyone. Take your time. Do things properly.

Once you have made improvement in your endurance you must continue to exercise regularly. Exercise has to be part of your weekly routine if you want to maintain your improved condition. The benefits are lost within a matter of weeks if you stop completely. If you must stop temporarily for a few days or a few weeks, always restart at a lower intensity level and take at least as much time to build up to your previous level as you were absent from your program.

Endurance training is intended to put a

healthy stress on your heart, lungs, and circulatory system. It is imperative that you have no medical problems which could be aggravated by this type of exercise.

If you are under 30 years of age and have no previous history of heart or lung problems, you can proceed as long as your doctor has examined you in the past ½ year and found that you are healthy. Between the ages of 30 and 50 you should have a recent medical check-up (within 3 months before exercising) that includes a ECG (electrocardiogram); and if you are above age 40, the ECG should also be done during exercise.

Above age 50 your medical checkup should be done immediately before beginning the exercise program. The importance of the medical check-up cannot be overemphasized.

Endurance exercising must be done gradually and progressively, the same way that you proceed gradually with strengthening and flexibility exercises. Endurance exercises should be as tailored to your individual needs as any other part of your Basic Program of exercise. It should represent your present abilities and your interests.

Ask yourself: what kind of skier am I?

What is my usual need for energy expenditure and endurance? Do I ski at an easy, nontaxing pace all of the time? Do I ski more aggressively and look for places to quicken my speed and make many more turns in a short distance? Would I like to be this kind of skier, but am not because I get too winded and have to stop too frequently?

Perhaps you've realized that you would like to become a stronger, tougher skier but you know that at present you don't have the stamina for it. Do you think that you're more like a marathon runner or more like a 100-yard sprinter? Perhaps your style is a combination of both.

Think of your training program as being as specifically tailored to your needs as any other part of your Basic Program of exercises. Remember, if you intend to ski as though you're jumping over hurdles, then by all means train yourself for it. If you need strong, sudden spurts of effort when you ski, be sure to add some type of sprinting to your endurance program.

As part of your total fitness program, you can do endurance exercises in the same session as the others or at another time of day. It doesn't make any difference. Choose activities that you enjoy and do them with a friend if that helps your motivation and enjoyment. However, remember that your needs and the needs of your friend may be very different although you are both about the same age. Your resting pulse rates may differ, or the intensity of work needed to get you to your target zone may differ. One of you may be able to endure much more activity than the other at the start. And remember, vary your activities from time to time so that you're not always doing the same thing throughout the whole year.

GUIDELINES

1. Endurance training should be done at least 3 times a week, not on consecutive days.

2. Each session begins with a warm-up of stretching and easy, active movements.

3. The stimulus period lasts 20 to 30 minutes. The intensity of the stimulus is increased gradually within each sesson and from session to session. Exercise during the stimulus period is in your target zone.

4. The stimulus is followed by a cool-down period to gradually taper off the intensity of the exercising.

5. Re-evaluation of progress is made every 4 weeks.

6. Endurance exercising should be regular, and carried out all year round.

7. Minimize muscular and joint injuries. Wear proper shoes and use soft running surfaces.

8. Observe the following precautions and stop exercising if you experience:

a. Severe breathlessness. Normal breathing of 12 to 16 breaths per minute should return within 10 minutes.

b. Lightheadedness

c. Dizziness

d. Chest pain or chest tightness

e. Loss of muscle coordination

f. Nausea

24 | Mini-Exercises

What are mini-exercises? These are easy but effective exercises that you can sneak in throughout the day. In many instances, no one else will know that you're exercising. This is not a substitute for regular exercising, but it is an effective way to boost your circulation and reduce fatigue which is caused by temporary or prolonged inactivity. Minis are a bonus that you give to yourself, not a replacement for your regular program.

A good time to do minis is whenever you're sitting in one place for more than an hour at a time (in your car driving or riding; at your desk; or watching television). Some exercises are isometric. Hold each position for 5 seconds, wait 5 seconds, then repeat several times. These are:

- Squeeze both knees together
- Squeeze buttocks together
- Pelvic tilt, pulling abdominal muscles inward
- Point both feet toward the ceiling
- Point both feet toward the floor
- Shrug both shoulders
- Squeeze both shoulder blades together

Remember that it is as important to relax the muscles completely between each repetition as it is to perform the isometric contraction. Repeatedly contracting and relaxing the muscles helps to reduce generalized fatigue because you use muscular activity to stimulate your blood circulation. If possible, get up and walk around to let the natural pumping action of the calf muscles aid the return of blood from your legs back up to your heart.

For a little more movement, repeat each of these movements 3 to 5 times:

- Quickly jiggle your knees inward and outward
- Swing your legs frontward and backward from the knees.
- Raise each thigh upward as if marching in place.
- Raise your arms in the air overhead, behind your neck and behind your back. Clasp your hands behind your head and move your elbows inward and outward. Repeat the entire sequence several times.
- Turn your head from side to side, trying to look as far as you can over each shoulder.
- If you are in your car or at a desk, move your car seat or desk chair backward to give your legs a chance to stretch out and change position. If you already sit very far away, move your seat closer for a change of position.
- If possible, use a chair with casters so that you can use your leg muscles throughout the day to push your chair around in your work area. (This is also advantageous for your lower back because it allows you to get closer to things in your work area without having to twist your spine to reach for them.)

For mini-stretching there are many places where you can place your foot on a low step or railing to stretch the calf and ankle. This is especially important for people who wear high-heeled shoes, which keep the foot in the down-ward, plantar flexed position. This position shortens the heel cord, which if not stretched out becomes chronically tight. A tight heel cord makes you more susceptible to "pulls" of the calf musculature.

The following mini-strengthener should not be done in the presence of strangers unless you don't mind being stared at. It's called the "Otis-Exercise" (alias, the Elevator-Mini). The way to do this one is to ring for an elevator, but if it doesn't come right away you have time to do the exercise.

Lean against the nearest smooth wall and do the wall sitting exercise. For how-to, see exercise 50. The first part of the exercise is to stay in position until the elevator arrives. The second part begins when you are in the elevator and the doors close, and you are planning to travel quite a few floors. For this, you must stay in position against the wall of the elevator until you reach your floor or another person steps into the elevator, whichever occurs first. (I must admit that although I do this exercise very often, I always stand up when someone else steps into the elevator.)

Another ideal time for wall sitting is during television commercials. Start practicing with 30-second commercials. That is, you must stay in position until the ad is completely over. Graduate to 1 minute of commercials and then to combinations of short and long commercials presented back-to-back as your strength and mental resolve increase. This is an exercise where you can see week-by-week improvement if you do it several times a day. It is a superb exercise for the thighs of downhill skiers.

25 ‖ The Skier and His Back

Skiers are active people. They enjoy physical activities and many participate in other sports in addition to skiing. Some people equate occasional physical participation with good physical conditioning. Their thinking is, "I'm active, I'm athletic, therefore I'm fit." Too often this kind of thinking leaves these people exceptionally vulnerable to some unexpected aches and pains. They're taking too much for granted.

Many people fall into this category of the "weekend athlete." They do little or no physical exercise during the week, then go all-out and expend themselves fully on the weekends. Exercising in spurts like this often leaves you suffering throughout the next week with a variety of complaints, one of the most frequent of which is the common backache.

In addition to the aches that come as a result of placing unusual stresses on an unprepared body are the disabling back pains that seem to come from doing nothing more strenuous than leaning over to pick up a small tote bag. The causes and prevention of this type of insidious back attack will be the subject of this chapter.

To get a general understanding of back ailments requires a brief look at the anatomy and mechanics of this part of the body. The lower part of the human spine, the lumbar region, is particularly vulnerable to stress. The structures depend on the integrity of strong and flexible muscles in the lower back and pelvis for their protection.

Normally there is a small degree of curvature in the lower back, which you can feel as the hollow in your low back when you stand with your back against a wall. The more exaggerated this curve, the more stress and strain is applied to the delicate structures of the spinal column. What are some of the most common causes of excessive back curvature?

The following factors contribute toward the excessive arching of the lower back:

1. Weak abdominal muscles
2. Tight hamstring muscles
3. Tight back extensor muscles
4. Tight hip flexion muscles
5. Faulty posture
6. Obesity

Let's examine these one by one to understand the low back mechanism.

1. *Abdominal Muscles* The abdominal muscles attach to the front of the pelvis. When they are strong, their contraction keeps the pelvis rolled backward and the lumbar arch to a minimum. This is the basis for the Pelvic Tilt, exercise 27. The weaker the abdominal muscles, the more the pelvis tips forward, and with it the lumbar spine moves forward. This could be the start of chronic backache.

2. *Tight Hamstring Muscles* These muscles attach from the rear edge of the pelvis to the back of the knee joint. When they are tight and in-

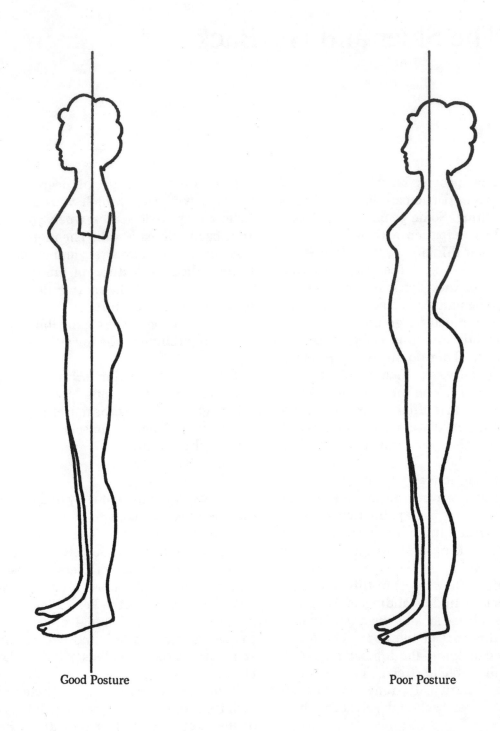

Good Posture   Poor Posture

flexible they restrict the tilting excursion of the pelvis and keep it in a forward tilted position. This, too, increases the lumbar curve.

3. *Tight Back Extensor Muscles* Lack of flexibility in this muscle group maintains the spine in the restrictive, arched position. When this is the case it is very difficult to bend forward at the waist because the back feels tight and stiff.

4. *Tight Hip Flexion Muscles* These muscles attach to the small bones (vertebrae) of the lumbar spine and to the inner side of the thigh bone. Tightness and lack of flexibility of these muscles creates a forward pulling force on the lower spine, again bringing the spine forward and increasing the lumbar curve.

5. *Faulty Posture* Any time that you stand with your knees fully extended, your lower back arched and your abdomen protruding, you are placing the lumbar spine in a position of potential stress. In this type of posture your body weight passes through the rear edges of your vertebrae and discs and creates uneven pressure on these structures; potentially harmful pressures.

Sleeping on your stomach places the lumbar spine in the exaggerated, arched position. Sitting slumped in a chair with both legs stretched out ahead, the pelvis tends to roll forward . . . the lumbar spine arches. When sitting, anytime that your knees are closer to the floor than your hips, the pelvis can tip forward. This is why it's easy to develop a backache sitting on a bar stool with both feet dangling below.

6. *Obesity* (and Pregnancy) This cause of backache is caused by the amount of weight carried in the front of the body and the resulting forward pull on the lumbar spine. The combination of weak and lax abdominal muscles with the frontal weight places a large demand on the small muscles of the lower back to keep the torso erect. This is a stress that these small,

back extensor muscles weren't designed to handle. The result? Your lower back feels tired and uncomfortable.

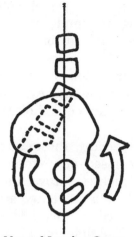

Normal Lumbar Curve

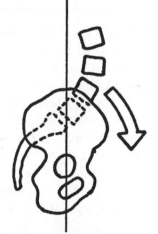

Pelvis Tipped Forward
Exaggerated Lumbar Curve

The weekend athlete, or any person, with one or more of the above muscular inadequacies may be walking a thin line between a pain-free and a painful back. If your back lacks resilience and the protection afforded by good musculature, all it takes is one instance of sudden stretch, even something as simple as pulling your skis off of the car rack, to bring on an incapacitating back pain. All it takes is a day of excessive emotional aggravation or tension to tighten your already tight muscles even more and leave you a victim of sudden and disabling back pain.

Long car drives, especially those anxious drives in bad weather, can set you up for a back muscle spasm at the slightest provocation if your muscles are already in a pre-tensed state.

What can be done to reduce the chances of this happening to you? The first step is to take the Physical Fitness Quiz, tests 1 through 6, and follow an exercise program so that you can pass each one of these tests without difficulty. The second step is to be aware of body positions that create potentially harmful forces in the lower spine.

The back extensor muscles in the lower spine are very small muscles which are not in a good position to exert a lot of strength. Therefore, if you bend over at your waist without bending your knees and rely on these small muscles to bring your torso back up to the upright position, you are placing a very large workload on them. If you reach over to pick something up, the force required to raise the body becomes even greater. In this situation, pressure is built within the spinal column (specifically within the discs that lie between each vertebrae). The small muscles and ligaments offer very little protection and the lumbar area is susceptible to severe strain.

The message here is to avoid placing your back in this situation. Do not lean over at the waist with your legs straight, creating a fulcrum at your lumbar spine. What you should do is reach down for things by bending your legs to lower your entire body. Keep your upper body close to the vertical, and let the bending of your legs lower you and the straightening of your legs raise you up again. If you carry or raise things when they are held out ahead of you (heavy objects or light but bulky objects), you are asking your lower back to sustain a workload that isn't well-suited for it. If you cannot hug something close to you to pick it up, you probably should not be attempting to lift it at all.

In summary, don't ruin a ski weekend or a ski vacation by allowing yourself to be a prime candidate for a sudden back strain. Keep yourself active throughout the year; active in ways that help, not harm, your back. Keep your muscles strong and flexible. Take the Physical Fitness Quiz and make sure that you can pass the first six tests. Be cautious when you reach for your equipment. Remember when you've been riding in the car or traveling in a bus to a ski area that your muscles may be a little tight and inflexible from prolonged inactivity. Follow the routine for slope-side limbering, Chapter 27, to reduce your chances of making a sudden move and not being able to move back again to the opposite direction.

26 || Optional Apparatus

The basic program outlined in this book is designed to be done at home with a minimum of exercise equipment. You may have exercise apparatus at home or have access to a gym or other health facility. If you have equipment at home, such as the popular and inexpensive cable and pulley sets that attach to a door knob, this chapter suggests ways of using it. The benefits are that it gives assistance to weak muscles and variety to your exercise program.

Obviously, one piece of equipment such as the pulley cannot be the answer to total physical fitness. This is the biggest limitation to the use of such units for "total" fitness. In fact, these units and many other commercially available exercise gadgets emphasize the strengthening of some muscular groups very heavily and exclude others entirely. The advantage of the pulley apparatus is that the pulling action by your arms assists the upward motions of your legs. In certain positions it also allows you to assist the stretching of the opposing muscles.

The kind of shoulder strengthening that you get from the arm pulling is limited because of the light weight involved and the fact that your arms travel only a very short distance. Usually, when shoulder and upper arm strength are required in skiing, you need to push your arms down and back behind you. The pulley unit doesn't incorporate these movements adequately. However, the arm cables can be used to assist you in maintaining a stretch on the hamstring muscles.

If you failed the Straight Leg Raising test, Chapter 9, and are doing corrective exercises for tight hamstrings, use the pulley when you get to the "Aerial Hamstring Stretch." Lie on your back with one cable loop around each foot and each hand. When your knee is fully extended in the air, keep it suspended there, with the stretching feeling behind your knee and thigh.

From the same position with your leg pointing up in the air you can slowly lower it toward the side, little toe toward the floor, to give an additional and different stretch, this time to the inner thigh muscles. (Bring your leg back inward to the upright position without the use of the cable and you're using the inner thigh muscles in a strengthening maneuver.)

The pulley unit can also help you to get started on abdominal and hip flexing exercises if you failed the Physical Fitness Quiz, tests 1 and 2. The more work you do with your arms, the less work your weak abdominal and hip flexing muscles do.

Use the pulley in the following way: Lie flat on your back, with one cable loop around each foot and each hand. Keep your knees fully extended on the floor, both hands pointing toward the ceiling. The action is to flex both knees *slowly* toward your chest, assisted by pulling both hands to the floor. *Slowly* return your legs to the starting position on the floor. Repeat this motion a few times, gradually increasing the number of repetitions in the same way you do for all of your basic exercises.

If you're able to perform several repetitions of the Sidelying Upper Leg Lift exercise 74 in good form, doing the same exercise with one set of pulleys can help build muscular strength in the hip abductor muscles. Follow the instructions for the exercise as written in the Basic Program. Add the use of your hand pulling down to the floor to help raise your leg. In addition, if you can pull your leg high enough to get a stretching sensation in your inner thigh, you are then stretching the adductor muscles.

Another piece of home exercise "apparatus" popularized by John Caldwell, Nordic trainer and Olympic Coach, in *Caldwell on Cross-Country* is the worn-out bicycle inner tube. The value of this type of exercise is that it closely approximates the direction of leg movements used in the forward leg drive in cross-country skiing.

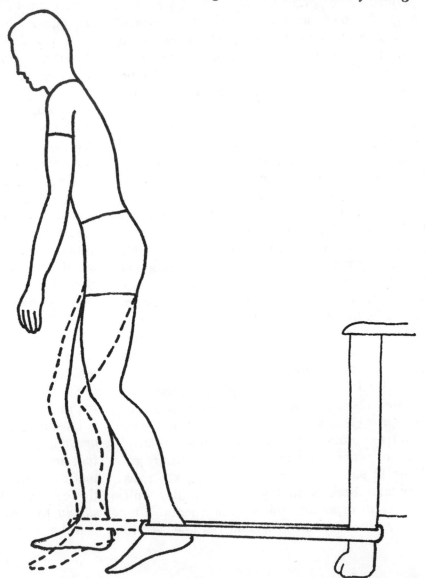

The procedure for this exercise is to loop the rubber inner tube around a secure stake in the ground or around the leg of a very sturdy and durable piece of furniture. Loop your ankle through the tubing. Then draw your leg forward sustaining the pull for 5 seconds, initiating the motion with your foot. Just a few of these leg pulls and you know that your muscles are doing some hard work, Start out with only a few repetitions for each leg to avoid excessive muscular soreness.

If you have access to an exercise facility equipped with Nautilus exercise apparatus, you can take advantage of this excellent system for physical training (Nautilus Sports/Medical Industries, De Land, Florida). More and more health clubs are installing this training system, which is already used by many professional athletic teams. The Nautilus system encourages muscular flexibility and strengthening in the same exercise. Different pieces of equipment allow you to exercise all the major muscles and joints of the body. It provides a large range of motion at the joints, and puts muscles into a pre-stretched position before the start of the contraction of these same muscles. This combination of stretching and strengthening has proven to be of great advantage in promoting muscular fitness. Nautilus exercise is high-intensity exercise, which means that you must work maximally, to the point of momentary fatigue in the muscle group, to derive the most benefit. Momentary fatigue means that you cannot do another repetition of the movement.

Nautilus apparatus is designed to provide resistance throughout the entire movement, from the starting position through the mid-range to the finishing position. This is in contrast to weight training, where most of the resistance is encountered in the first part of the motion and momentum helps carry the weight through to the completion of the movement. For overall conditioning, weight training is less satisfactory than a full range resistance system.

In Nautilus, your movements are done at a steady pace that allows your muscles to work hard at all times. On an average, you would do only 8 to 12 repetitions for each muscle group and complete a total session for the whole body in 30 to 40 minutes. Two or three sessions a week is all that is recommended. Endurance exercising for the cardio-respiratory system should be added to round out the program.

27 | Ski Lodge and Slope-Side Warm-Ups

You've probably seen professional athletes doing warm-up exercises before a game or event begins. A proper warm-up is essential for them to perform at their best and to reduce the risk of injury from straining tight muscles.

There are many opportunities for you to do the same thing with a few simple stretches when you arrive at the ski area. You can't expect to do your best if you've been sitting in your car driving to the ski area, then put on your boots, grab your gear and bound up to the lift line without getting your muscular system somehow prepared for the physical activities of the day. There's no reason that you shouldn't give yourself every advantage, much as any professional athlete does.

Before your first ski run, even before you put your skis on, a few minutes of stretching can help you to feel more limber and ready to ski. A few minutes of these exercises starts to increase your body metabolism, which means that your muscular system will be performing at a better level.

Inside the ski lodge: (The figures in parentheses refer to exercises in the Basic Program)

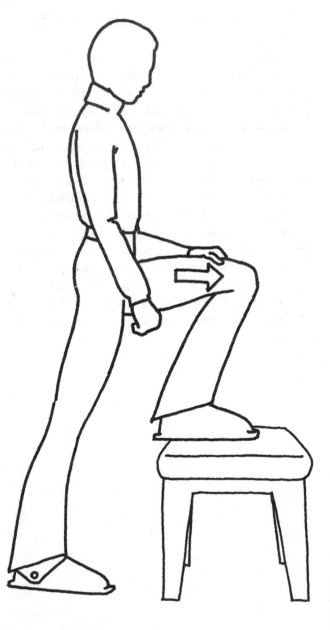

• Place one foot up on a nearby chair seat or bench. Feel a gentle stretch in the calf and back of the thigh when you lean forward. (53)

• Place one foot up on a bench or chair and feel a stretch on the front of the hip of the opposite leg.

• Clasp both hands behind you, lift them behind your back to squeeze the shoulder blades together, and stretch the front of the shoulders and chest. (4)

• Sit on the edge of a chair or bench, and bend forward to touch your fingertips to the floor between your feet. (33)

• Grasp one ankle and bring the foot toward your buttock to stretch the front of the thigh. (46)

After you have put your skis on, stretch some more to loosen up. Some of the movements are like the movements you do on the slope. They help you to get into the feeling of skiing before you start downhill. Whenever you do these exercises, be sure that you have plenty of room, away from the other skiers and pedestrians.

• Reach down to touch the front of your boots. Keep your knees as straight as your boots will allow. (38)

• Place the poles together and grasp them with one hand at the hand grip end and the other hand at the basket end. Lift your arms overhead. Then bend sideways as far as you can to the right and left to feel the stretch in the side of your torso. (19)

• Hold the poles horizontally in front of you. Crouch down as far as you can, stretching the poles ahead of you. Rise back up to the standing position, maintaining the poles in the same position.

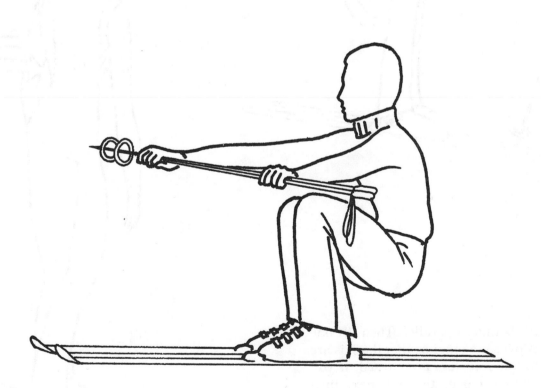

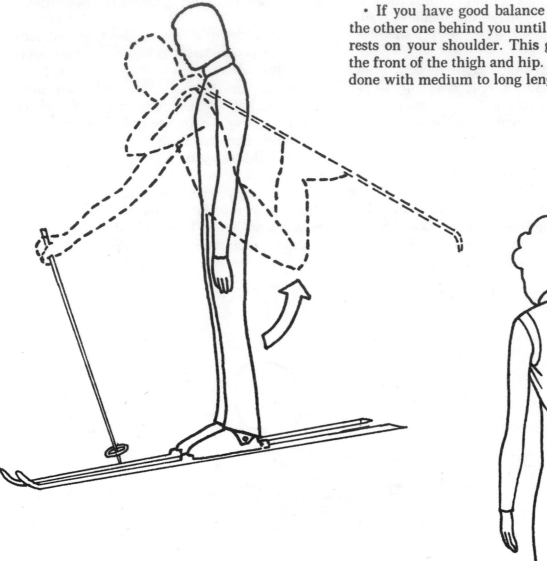

• If you have good balance on one ski, raise the other one behind you until the tail of the ski rests on your shoulder. This gives a stretch to the front of the thigh and hip. (This can only be done with medium to long length skis.)

• Stand with both skis parallel. Then lift one ski completely over the other so that the skis are again parallel, but your legs are crossed, If you crossed the right ski over the left, next turn your upper body as far as you can to the right to stretch your trunk muscles.

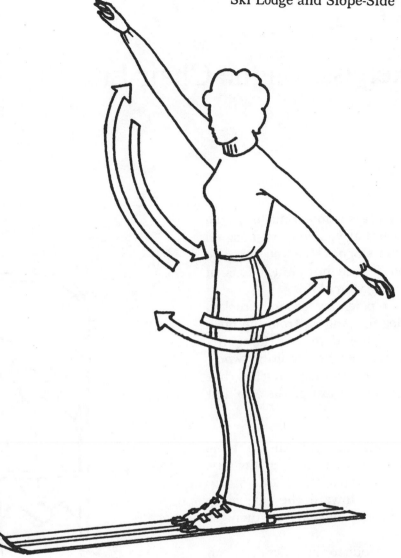

• Without poles, swing your arms in big circles in the air, both clockwise and counterclockwise.

• Without poles, swing your arms forward and backward.

• Finally, run in place with skis on. Alternately and quickly, raise the tails of the skis, leaving the tips on the snow.

Before starting down the slope on my first run of the day, I always like to take a few moments after getting off the lift to "remind" my legs of what they're going to be doing. I hop in place from one ski to the other, placing them close together to finish each hop. I start with the skis far apart and gradually bring them closer and closer together with each hop. The next maneuver is to wiggle the knees from side to side, keeping the skis parallel. Finally, I do a few shuffles in place, alternately sliding the skis forward and backward, then a kick turn, and I descend the slope.

28 | Exercises on the Chair Lift

Riding on the chair lift is a good time to stretch some of the muscles that you've been using on your runs down the slope. Once you begin to stretch you'll soon realize how much tension you've built up during your skiing.

Be sure that your poles are securely tucked underneath your leg or hanging from the hook provided for that purpose. If you are riding in a two or four-person gondola, you probably won't have enough room to do the leg stretches, but you can probably manage most of the arm and neck stretches.

• Turn your head all the way to the right and left. Stretch your head up to look at the sky; tuck your chin down toward your chest.
• Reach your hands toward the sky; clasp them together overhead and stretch them as high as you can.
• Spread your arms out to the sides. You can place one arm on the top of the chair back, but be careful not to knock off your partner's hat in the process.
• Place your hands behind your head and spread your elbows as far apart as you can.
• If you're not too bundled with heavy clothing, try the Triceps Stretch. (8)

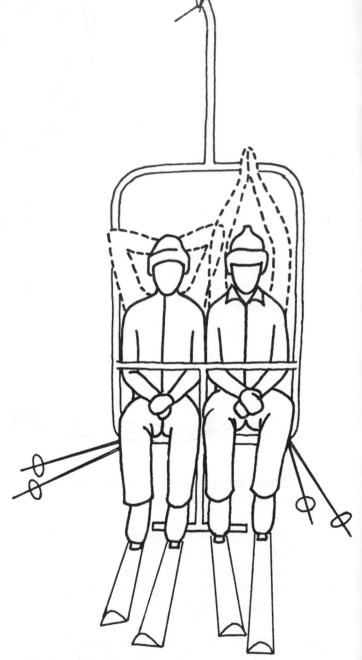

• Stretch one leg at a time out straight in front of you. Carefully swing one ski tip in an arc from right to left by rolling your foot and leg inward and outward.

• Keep both skis parallel, with your legs dangling, and twist both skis simultaneously from right to left.

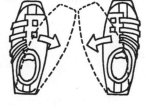

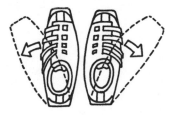

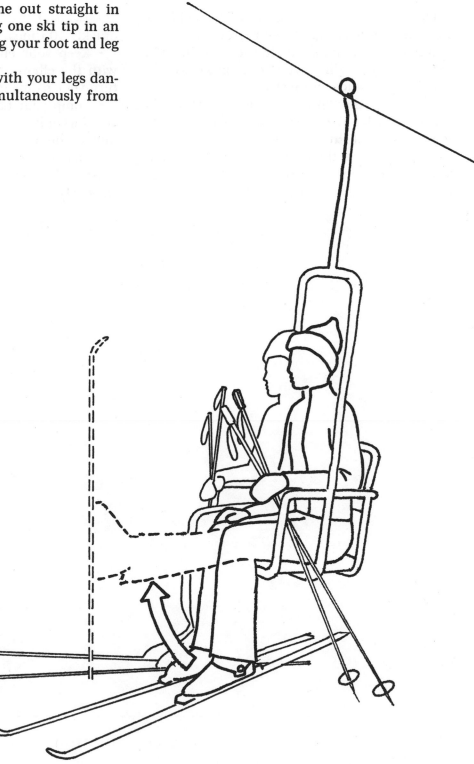

On very cold days, it's useful to do the following exercises to stimulate your circulation while you're relatively immobile in the chair lift. Finger and toe wiggling are always good, too, for keeping the hands and feet warm.

• Squeeze the buttocks together. Hold the contraction for a few seconds, then relax the tension. Repeat this rapidly 10 times.

• Squeeze the thighs together and then release the tension. Hold for a few seconds each time and repeat rapidly 10 times.

• Jiggle both knees inward and outward quickly 10 times.

• Keep your elbows tucked in at your sides with the elbows bent to a right angle. Briskly turn your palms upward and downward.

• Pump your hands up and down rapidly by bending only at the elbows (see elbow flexion illustration in Chapter 13). Alternately touch each hand to your knee and to your shoulder. Raise and lower the arms alternately or simultaneously.

29 | Relaxation on the Slope

When we think of relaxation we think of getting our ski boots off, wiggling our feet around, and especially on those January days in the Northeast, eagerly waiting for the circulation and warmth to return to our fingers and toes!

Did you know that you don't have to save up all your relaxation time until the end of the ski day? There are ways to relax your body and your mind while you're out on the mountain. One way to relax your body is to give it the opportunity to do a variety of things during the day. For example, you can spend part of your morning skiing on relatively steep, fast slopes, where you are making many tight turns, and then switch over to terrain that lets you make more moderate, wider turns. Find a run that lets you make long-radius, sweeping arcs across the slope while making as few turns as possible.

Take notice of the way you've been skiing. Hands held high? Let them come down lower for a while. Have you been skiing in a very low position? Then change your style to make it a bit more erect. You can always crouch into a racer's tuck and relax your neck, back, and arms. Do you hold your breath when you're skiing? Do you ski down, come to a stop and rapidly gasp for air? Try to remember to breathe continuously, openly and freely while you ski. It helps to relax your entire body and encourages you to move with greater freedom and ease.

While on the slope you can stop for a few minutes along the side of a trail, stretch your arms and legs, and loosen up your neck. Excessive tension in your neck tends to set up a tension reaction throughout the whole body. You need a mobile head to react quickly to sudden changes in direction and to be able to look around the slope at where you're going.

You can also take a few minutes to do some mental relaxing. For this, find a place out of the way of skier traffic. Ideally, there should be as little noise as possible. Close your eyes, take a few deep breaths, and begin to feel your body lighten and relax. Leave your arms hanging comfortably at your sides.

Imagine and visualize each part of your body. Toes, feet, ankles, calves, knees, thighs, hips, fingers, hands, forearms, elbows, shoulders, neck, back, and stomach. As your mind concentrates on each part, feel that the part gets lighter and lighter, losing its tension. Also relax your forehead and eyes and mouth.

Now that your body is less tense, try to clear your mind of all thoughts except for the vision of a clean, white slate in front of your eyes. You look at the white, empty surface and at first you don't see anything at all. Then you begin to make out the figure of a skier moving down and across the white surface. Imagine that this skier is the best skier that you know, or a skier whose style you admire very much. As you watch this skier you see him make very wide, carving turns that are very easy and very gentle. As he continues to ski he proceeds through some small bumps, turning on the back of the bumps and also on top of some of them. You continue to watch him as if you are skiing about 50 feet behind him. You imagine that not only are you behind him but that you are skiing in the tracks that he made, making the same type of turns that he made. As you watch yourself skiing behind him you can see that the distance between you gets smaller and smaller until you are skiing closer and closer to him, always staying in the same tracks, always making the same kind of graceful, smooth turns. You follow closely behind him in packed snow and light fluffy powder, in sweeping turns and tight turns. Finally, your body merges with his and his movements become your movements. Ski as he skis for a few moments. And then, when you've watched yourself in your mind's eye skiing better than you've ever skied before, open your eyes, take your poles in hand, and head down the slope. See if you don't really enjoy the next run.

30 || Après-Ski Relaxation

When you're at home or at your lodge after skiing you can do relaxation exercises. Many people feel that after skiing the last thing they want to do is more exercise, but relaxation exercises usually bring renewed energy. It's tough to get started, but the results are immediate and very satisfying. It's particularly nice to feel re-energized if you're planning to go out in the evening after resting for a while indoors.

You can start by elevating your feet for a few minutes. They should be high in the air, resting on a chair or other object so that your feet are above the level of your chest. For maximum elevation, lie on the floor or bed and lean your legs against the wall (exercise 66). To incorporate a stretching to the back of the legs and get your feet as high as possible, keep your buttocks and the entire back of your legs against the wall. To get into this position you will have to lie on your side close to the wall, make buttock contact with the wall and then swing your legs up to the vertical position. To lower the legs after a few minutes of elevation, bend your knees toward your chest and then drop them over toward one side.

When your legs are in the vertical position against the wall, you can work on some other stretches for the inner thighs and back of the legs. Try to do the Variations of the exercise, Adductor Stretch, Backlying, 66, if you are flexible in this region. Follow up the wall routine with the floor routine of Limbering Exercises, Chapter 11.

In the first couple of days after skiing you may become aware of muscular soreness and aching in just about any part of your body. Most likely you will feel it in any of the following places: upper arms, below the shoulder blades, in the front of the thighs, shins and calves. You can learn from these aches. They may be telling you where you should have built up more strength or flexibility.

ACHES

Aches may also be telling you something about your skiing style. Increased tension in the shin may be a clue that you've been leaning backward too much. Notice if, when you ski, you feel your toes come up to the top inside of the boot. Excessive tension in the buttock on one side may suggest unequal distribution of your weight over the skis, with weight bearing on one leg more than the other. Does this correspond to your being able to turn better to one side than the other?

Is your upper or lower back stiff? You may not be flexible enough for the many balancing adjustments you need to make; or you may be leaning far forward with your head and upper trunk.

Any of these localized aches can be managed with the specific, gentle stretches found in this book for that region of the body. In the warm water of a bathtub or whirlpool bath you can begin gentle stretching movements. Then continue them out of the water. Wait until most of the soreness is gone before you restart vigorous, strengthening routines for a very sore muscle.

If you have a tense, tight muscle that you can't stretch at all due to severe discomfort (and the possibility of a serious underlying injury has been ruled out), you should try ice massage. This procedure will be found in the Appendix. Its purpose is to allow you to begin very gentle stretching that you could not do previously because of severe discomfort.

31 || Shiatsu Therapy for Skiers

Relaxation after strenuous physical exercise, such as after a day of skiing, is an important part of good physical conditioning. Stiffness, heaviness, and fatigue in specific parts of your body can be reduced by the use of Shiatsu, Japanese finger pressure therapy. Shiatsu, derived from the Japanese characters for fingers (shi) and pressure (atsu) is a form of massage that you can apply to yourself or have applied to you by a partner.

Shiatsu is based on a system of body zones, called *meridians,* and local points, called *tsubo.* These are invisible areas on the surface of the body. They have been located in approximately. the same location for each person and have been systematically charted. Applying pressure at the tsubo or rubbing an area along a particular meridian is said to release the flow of bodily energy through parts of the body related to those points. In many instances, the tsubo is located at a place quite far from the body organ that it serves. Practically speaking, treatment at the points relieves the symptoms of muscular fatigue and overuse at that location and at other sites or body organs along the same meridian.

When something hurts us we automatically react by rubbing the area with our hands. This is considered the origin of Shiatsu therapy. Applying finger and thumb pressure at points on the back and legs constitutes a basic treatment for skiers who suffer aches and stiffness along the sides of the trunk, below the shoulder blades, in the thighs, calves, and knees. Shiatsu stimulates the skin and underlying muscles, stimulates blood circulation and other body fluids, and soothes irritated nerve endings.

Keichi Murata, an experienced Shiatsu therapist in New York City who is also a skier, suggests that the most effective Shiatsu is applied by a partner. In this way, pressure can be applied vertically through the fingers toward the center of the body or limb. The person who gives the treatment can lean his body weight through the pressure of his fingers more effectively than he could with pressure of the fingers alone. Shiatsu given to yourself can also be effective, but good vertical pressure is more difficult to achieve and it just isn't as relaxing as having someone else do it to you.

Shiatsu for the back, which can only be done working with a partner, will be discussed first. Study the hand positions illustrated in the figures. Notice that although the hands may be resting on the body, all of the pressure in these finger techniques is directed through the fingertips or thumb tips. The Shiatsu technique is to keep your fingers in contact with the skin throughout the pressure or rubbing phase and move the skin over the muscles. Your fingers do not slide over the skin as in a conventional, stroking massage.

To the person receiving Shiatsu, certain points will be much more sensitive than others. In fact, they may be exquisitely tender. These

points should receive special attention, for this is where the energy flow through the meridian has been interrupted. The most tender tsubo are where you need Shiatsu the most. You will see that one point on your body feels like nothing more than the dull pressure of someone's finger pressing there, while another point just millimeters away is remarkably sensitive to even moderate pressure.

TIGHT BACK AND TIRED ARMS?

The treatment area should be padded but very firm. Use a low table or the floor. The person taking the Shiatsu lies flat on his stom-

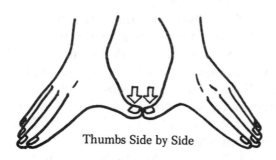

Thumbs Side by Side

Thumbs Overlapping

ach with no pillow or only a very small one under the head. The head must be completely relaxed and the chest in full contact with the padded surface.

For the back, the side-by-side thumb technique is used, except that the thumbs are spread apart so that each thumb is 1½ inches to the side of the spine.

Step 1. Place each thumb on point 1, line 1. This point is level with the upper edge of the shoulder blade. The point is on the muscle between the shoulder blade and the spine.

Step 2. Keep your elbows fully extended and apply pressure, good firm pressure, for 3 seconds. Straddling your partner will put you in the best position to apply firm, vertical pressure.

Step 3. Move your thumbs to point 2, line 1. Apply pressure again for 3 seconds at these points and at each of the 10 remaining points on the back. The points are approximately 1 inch apart; some people may have as many as 14 in total.

Step 4. Repeat the same procedure on line 2, starting with point 1 and ending with point 12.

Step 5. Repeat this entire sequence on lines 1 and 2 three times.

SORE, STIFF THIGHS?

The following Shiatsu can be done on yourself or by a partner. Keep your knee flexed or extended, whichever is more comfortable.

Step 1. Place one thumb on the front thigh muscle on line 1, point 1.

Step 2. Apply pressure for 3 seconds at point 1 and each of the other four points.

Step 3. When you locate a very tender point, use your thumb to massage it in a circular motion. Keep your thumb in contact with your skin and move the skin over the thigh muscle.

Step 4. Next, place both thumbs together and press on each of the five points in the middle of the thigh from top to bottom on line 2.

Step 5. Repeat this entire sequence three times.

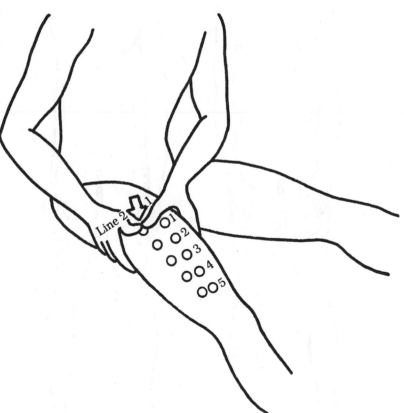

Next, stand with your hands loosely at your sides. Locate the points where your fingertips end on the front and sides of your thighs. Mr. Murata advises that these points are often very tender in skiers. They should be rubbed for one minute with circular massage with the thumbs or with the middle three fingers.

If you feel fatigue or discomfort in the area just above your kneecap, follow this procedure.

Step 1. Locate the point in the hollow, just below the bulk of the outer contour, of the thigh muscle. To locate this point easily, first tense your thigh to see the muscle definition. Keep your muscle totally relaxed when doing the Shiatsu.

Step 2. Use circular massage for one minute at this point. Use the pad of your thumb or the middle joint of your index finger.

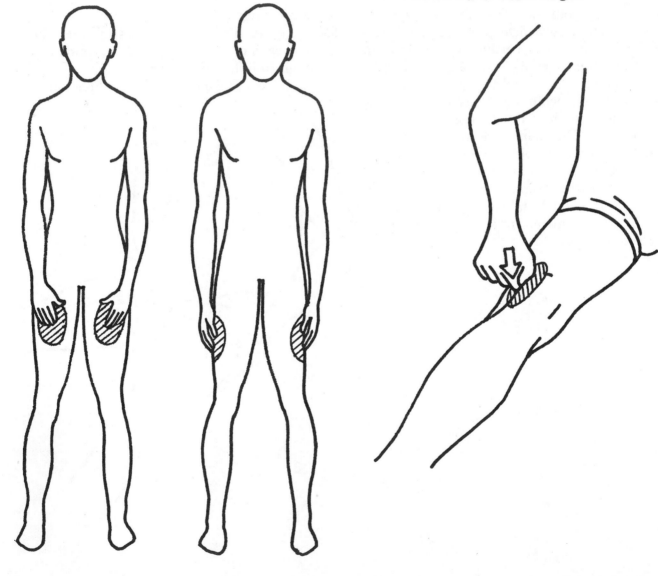

TIRED KNEES?

Step 1. Standing, locate the area where the crease of your groin reaches the outer side of your hip. Use your three middle fingers to do one minute of circular massage in this area (A). *Step 2.* Sitting down, locate the region just above each knee on the inside of the thighs (B). Use the three middle fingers to apply the same type of circular pressure and massage for one minute.

Tension in these two areas relates to the function of a particular muscle that begins at the outer side of the hip and crosses over the thigh to the inner side of the knee. Mr. Murata tells his skiing clients to release the tension in these areas just *before* going out to ski. With firm pressure it can be done right over your ski pants.

Do you find that you have tenderness in these places before skiing? If so, you should be sure to take it easy on the first few runs. Give yourself a good warm-up with general stretches and take some easy ski runs before tackling the more challenging ones.

ACHING IN THE LOWER LEGS?

Step 1. To locate points in the lower leg, slide your hand lightly up the outer side of your shin bone until you meet a bony projection on your leg, an inch or two below the kneecap. This is your starting point (C). *Step 2.* Using your thumb pad or middle thumb joint, press on this point and two points lower for 3 seconds each. Each of these points is four fingers' width apart. (If a partner is doing this for you, he can use overlapping thumbs). Repeat 3 times.

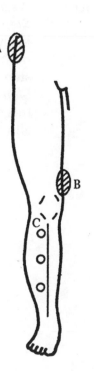

Are you having difficulty getting to sleep after skiing? Find the area that is three fingers' width above the inner ankle bone (D). Apply circular massage for one minute to this area. Use touching or overlapping thumbs. Do this for both legs, massaging the more sensitive one first.

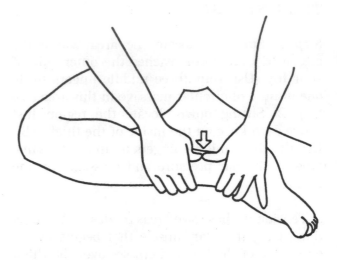

CRAMPING OR PAIN IN THE CALF?

The most important point on the calf is located in the center of the calf at the lower border of the calf muscle bulk.

Step 1. Find this point by tensing your calf and placing your thumb at this point (E).
Step 2. Use one thumb pad and press firmly for 3 seconds.
Step 3. Move your contact to points 1, 2 & 3 just below the knee at one inch intervals, pressing down to the center point that you pressed in step 2.
Step 4. Continue to press on points 4, 5, 6 from this center point along the outer side of your leg all the way to the ankle joint.

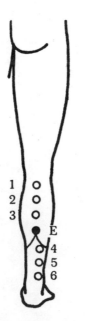

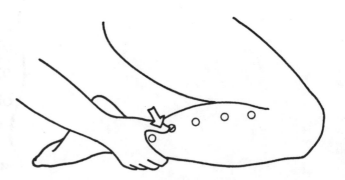

TOTAL LEG FATIGUE?

Step 1. Locate the tsubo on the inner aspect of the ankle in the depression just below your inner ankle bone.

Step 2. Apply light circular pressure on this point with the middle joint of your index finger for one minute.

Step 3. Move your contact over to the outer side of your ankle to the depression on that side of the ankle. Apply light circular pressure for one more minute.

Use your thumb for steps 2 and 3 if it is much easier for you.

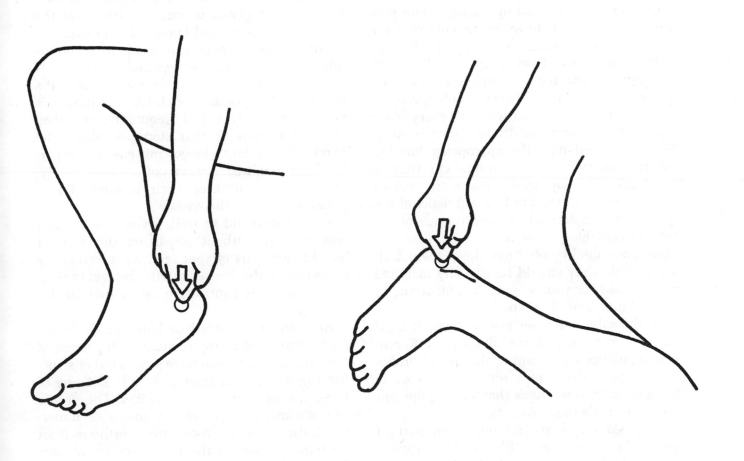

32 || Prevention of Ski Injuries

Many skiers have asked, "What can I do to prevent an injury?" As long as people ski there will be people falling, but the risk of sustaining an injury can be reduced by taking certain precautions. You can have some control over whether you have a high or low risk for injury.

Let's take a look at ski equipment. The most important feature for your safety is that your equipment be a compatible boot-binding system. Not every boot can be paired with every binding. Ski brakes and anti-friction devices must also be matched with the appropriate binding system. Always buy your equipment from a knowledgeable shop where there are trained mechanics who understand the subtleties of the equipment and can advise you on acceptable and unacceptable combinations.

Buy good quality bindings. Keep them well maintained. They should be properly mounted and adjusted for your weight, height, strength, skiing ability, and ski boots.

For the safety of other skiers always use ski brakes or run-away straps. Ski areas differ in their regulations concerning the use of brakes (some require that straps must be used while riding open lifts) so check that your equipment meets the area's requirements.

Sharp ski edges are an important part of proper ski maintenance. Skis with sharpened edges hold better on icy surfaces and carve turns more precisely. These metal edges are also a potential hazard. Most of your body is pro-

tected by ski clothing; if you fall and the ski comes loose, the parts of you that are protected by clothing are less likely to be harmed. Beware of very short gloves or mittens that leave the inside of the wrist and lower forearm exposed. A cut by the ski edge can result in a serious injury to the delicate nerves and blood vessels close to the surface of the skin in this area. It's particularly important for children to have this protection, for they fall frequently, and they often wear mittens that stop just above the hand. Give children longer mittens or use parkas with long inside wrist cuffs. Alternatively, instruct them to keep their sweater sleeves pulled down over the wrist.

Ski boots should fit well, giving you support and comfort without impairing the flow of blood to any part of your feet. Advanced skiers often rely on the fine sensitivity they get in their feet to precisely control the use of their ankles for edging.

Are you knock-kneed or bow-legged? Podiatrists estimate that approximately 80 percent of the general population have some kind of structural problem with their feet or legs. Some of these can be a problem for skiers. The proper use of cants (wedges placed inside or underneath the boots) or custom-made orthoses (foot appliances made for the exact contours of your foot) can be put inside the ski boots for better leg-foot-boot-ski alignment. You may have one leg that is slightly longer than the other or one leg that turns inward or outward more than the other. If uncorrected, these differences can affect your skiing, making it difficult for you to turn or edge in one particular direction or causing you to fall more often than you should.

The remainder of your ski outfit should fit comfortably and allow you to move your arms and legs freely in all directions. Your skiing will be freer and easier if your clothing lets you move without restriction and doesn't reduce the blood supply to your extremities. When the weather is cold, your body has enough of a job to keep you warm without the added difficulty of compensating for diminished blood flow because of too tight elastic bands at the wrists, waist, or ankles.

Use common sense, be honest with yourself, and you lower the risk of injury. Know what your limitations are. Statistics show that most injuries occur after two hours of skiing and late in the day. Stop skiing when you feel fatigued. *Ski where you belong, not where your friends think you should go.*

Physical conditioning retards muscular fatigue. Trained muscles lose their energy supply of glycogen less quickly and accumulate lactic acid more slowly than untrained muscles. With endurance training, the circulation of blood from your heart to your muscles is improved; then the muscular system has a better supply of oxygen and other nutrients.

Beginning skiers tend to use more static body positions than more experienced skiers. Their muscles are more stationary, contracting and relaxing far less than those of the more advanced "dynamic" skiers. It has been suggested that the decrease in nutritive blood flow to static muscles may be a contributing factor to muscular fatigue and falls. Therefore, when you're skiing, note when you're being "static." Change your skiing style. Use more action in your legs. Stop on the side of a slope away from the flow of skiers and move your legs around actively, or

take your skies off at the bottom of the slope and walk around for a short while. There is no rule in skiing that says that once your skis are on you have to keep them on and ski until you're ready to collapse. You may feel that you want to get your money's worth, as the price of a lift ticket goes higher and higher each year. However, be sensible; listen to your body's fatigue signals. Keep yourself skiing, not recuperating.

Many studies have also indicated that skiers who take lessons have fewer injuries. With good skills you're not only going to enjoy skiing more, but you're going to have a reduced chance of being seriously hurt.

Some skiers experience leg fatigue that disappears after a brief rest period riding the ski lift. If you have a variety of lifts to choose from, choose your lift with a rest period in mind. Look for chair lifts with foot rests. If unsupported, the weight of the skis can exert a pulling force on your feet which in some cases impairs the normal flow of blood to the feet. In addition, the resulting pressure on the back of your thighs and knees from the chair edge can reduce the flow of blood to your legs. Choose padded chairs over the hard-edged type, especially when there is no foot rest.

If you have been in a chair lift with no foot rest, ski down the ramp and wait a couple of minutes before skiing to restore good circulation. When sitting in a gondola or standing in a tram with your skis off you can sometimes stretch your legs or at least move them up and down to stimulate the circulation. In some ski areas you can take a T-Bar lift as conveniently as a chair lift to the top of the slope. Take advantage of the time on the T-Bar to shuffle your legs front and back, flex and extend your knees, alternately raise the tail of each ski, and shift your weight from side to side, from one leg to the other.

After sitting for a while, having lunch or sunning, you are relaxed both mentally and physically. If you're merely relaxed but not fatigued, activate your muscles again before skiing. Walk around for a while. Stretch your arms and legs. Do some of the Slope-Side Warm-Up exercises (Chapter 27).

Courteous skiing is safer skiing. Look uphill before you start down to make sure that you're not starting out directly in front of another skier. Slow down when you ski into congested areas, especially at the junction of two or more trails.

Keep physically fit throughout the year so that you are not getting into adequate shape somewhere toward the middle or end of the ski season. Remember that if you've had a ski injury or any other injury in the off-season, you must recondition yourself fully before skiing again.

33 || Rehabilitation of Injuries

Injury is not a subject that healthy skiers like to think about, but one nice thing about skiing injuries is that most of them heal very well and the skier goes back to skiing again. While the less severe injuries heal relatively quickly, the more complicated may take weeks or months to recover completely. In any case, there are some things to remember and some guidelines to follow to speed up your recovery.

One of the biggest delays in getting full recovery has more to do with the secondary muscle weakness and joint stiffness than with the original injury itself. When you remember that the healing period usually involves some kind of immobilization with a cast, splint, or traction you can see how easily muscles can become weakened from disuse; and the joints that frequently have to be kept still can become stiff from lack of motion. There are ways to rehabilitate yourself and keep prolonged disability to a minimum, starting soon after your injury has occurred.

Some people falsely believe that rehabilitation is a process that begins only after the injury is healed. Rehabilitation begins much earlier in the healing period. It involves the prevention of weakness in other parts of your body by doing stretching and strengthening exercises throughout the recovery period. There are exercises that can and should be done even if you are in leg traction. Rehabilitation means that you have to make special efforts to remember to use joints and muscles that aren't getting their normal dose of exercise when another part of the same extremity is temporarily out of commission. Rehabilitation also includes encouraging muscular work of the injured part with isometric exercises when immobilization prevents active motions.

A skier with a broken wrist may have a short cast covering his hand and forearm. Since the cast prevents him from using his fingers in the normal way to grasp, lift, and carry things, he should remember to wiggle his fingers frequently. Although he has no injury to his elbow or shoulder, he has fewer opportunities to use them in the normal way. Therefore, the muscles around those joints may become weak from lack of use. The homework for this skier is to remember to bend and straighten his elbow, raise his hand above his head, behind his neck, behind his back, out to the side, and across to the opposite shoulder. (Refer to the Anatomy drawings in Chapter 13 to remind yourself of the movements of the arm.) Shoulder shrugging and stretching exercises will help to maintain good function all around the shoulder and shoulder blades.

Let's look at another skier with a slightly different problem. This skier has injured his shoulder and has his arm immobilized in a sling. He has had little opportunity to use his hand in daily activities since his arm is kept alongside of his chest. It's important for him to maintain his hand mobility and forearm strength by squeezing a ball or clay or any one of a number of commercially available hand exercisers. He must not forget to move his wrist in all directions and to turn his palm to face both up and down.

The importance of staying as active as possible cannot be overemphasized. As long as you are ambulatory you should walk as much as possible, even if it feels slightly awkward or clumsy. Be especially careful crossing streets, for you may not turn as much as usual to the right and left. If you are using crutches, build up your stamina with them by taking many short but frequent walks throughout the day. (Consult the Appendix at the end of this book for some hints on walking with crutches.) And remember, until you can walk without any limp, you should use some form of hand support such as crutches or a cane.

Keeping up with your hamstring stretches, even if it is only for one uninjured leg, is beneficial. Continue to do abdominal strengthening and many other exercises for general conditioning to help you feel more energetic in your mind and body. In the section of this book on "mini-exercises," you will find some suggestions on doing muscular strengthening and stretching that can be adapted for use when more vigorous exercises aren't possible.

Whether you have broken or dislocated a bone, strained ligaments or torn tendons, remember that rehabilitation exercises are designed to:

1. Redevelop the strength of muscles weakened from injury or disuse.
2. Restore the elasticity of structures that have become stiff and tight from lack of motion, and
3. Restore full mobility of the joints.

Keep in mind also that the same principles apply to injuries sustained in the off-season as well as during the skiing season.

Complete recovery means that you have normal mobility in the joints and that the muscular system has as much strength and endurance as the opposite arm or leg. If you try to go back to skiing before the motion and strength are normal, you're asking for trouble. Not only do you chance reinjuring the same structures, which are now more vulnerable to stress, but you risk harming yourself in some other way because your balance and timing are off. Your reaction time in preventing falls may be slowed. Many injuries reoccur because the skier doesn't recondition himself adequately before he goes back to the slopes.

Always follow the advice of your doctor, who will tell you not only when to begin active exercising but what type of exercises he wants you to do. If you are fortunate enough to have a physical therapist in your community, you can receive expert guidance and assistance in many aspects of exercise. If you'll be exercising alone, you can show the exercises in this book to your doctor so that he may select the appropriate ones for you. Initially, your exercises will stress active motions, that is, using your own muscular strength to move a part of your body. Various forms of heat or cold can be used to make the early stages of active exercising go more easily.

Heat or cold can be used to make exercising the injured part more comfortable, but the use of either by itself without the exercises is of little value. (Immediately after an injury, within the first 48 hours, always apply cold to minimize swelling.) After your injury is healed and exercises are under way, first try heat. If you get no relief, try cold. In most cases, one or the other will be helpful. At home you can use a moist electric pad (use only those electric pads designed specifically for this purpose) or moist heat packs, known as hydrocollator packs. For your safety in applying heat, always follow the instructions that come with any heating device carefully and avoid heat over any part of the body that lacks normal sensation or normal blood supply. These convenient types of superficial heat produce a temporary, localized increase in blood circulation to the area, help in the relaxation of muscle fibers, and give you an overall feeling of relaxation that is beneficial before exercising.

There are commercially available creams and ointments which, when rubbed into the skin, produce the sensation of warmth. These, too, provide no real benefit unless, having used them, you are able to perform exercises that you wouldn't have done without them. A word of caution: never apply another type of heat, such as a heating pad, over an area of the skin that has already been covered with a "heat" producing cream.

A heated swimming pool or whirlpool bath is an excellent way to start active exercises. The warmth helps in relaxation, and the water's bouyancy supports the limb, making active movements easier.

With cold, applied as an ice pack or ice massage, you get a temporary anesthetic effect. It reduces pain and muscle spasm and allows you to stretch tense muscles more effectively. (Refer to appendix B in the back of the book for instructions for ice massage.)

Later, when you are able to do more difficult exercises, you will incorporate resisted movements to gain further strength. These are done with the manual resistance of a therapist or with exercise weights or other apparatus. The first goal, however, is to gain back the ability to move the part through its full excursion and then develop full strength. Your doctor may suggest some stretching movements to encourage greater muscle elasticity and joint motion, but these should be avoided in the very beginning, unless specifically indicated. In many cases a therapist can help you obtain the complete, normal joint "play" that you cannot obtain by exercising on your own, using special techniques of joint mobilization. Often the joint stiffness that accompanies injury can be alleviated by the therapist's manual application of pressure to restore full joint mobility.

Injuries that appear to be the same may be quite different. A doctor should diagnose the nature and seriousness of your particular injury. In fact, if you are injured at the ski area and are examined by the physician on duty at the ski patrol office, it's a good idea to have yourself re-examined when you get home if your symptoms don't improve. In many cases, an injury cannot be fully evaluated immediately after it occurs because of swelling and severe discomfort.

Just as your daily exercise program reflects your individual needs, so, too, your rehabilitation exercises must be specific. There is a tendency for people to swap stories and compare notes with others about their injuries. The exercises that were good for your friend may not be proper for you. It's not a good idea to follow the exercise regime of another person unless you check it with your doctor. Your age, general state of health, and the condition of your joints and muscles are but a few of the factors that make each case different from every other, even though the injuries may have occurred in the same way.

REHABILITATION EXERCISES

The following section is devoted to commonly prescribed rehabilitation exercises. Since these exercises are to be done during and after recovery from an injury, caution should be your primary concern. A common mistake is thinking that an exercise must be difficult or strenuous to be effective. Similarly, many people feel that if an exercise is painful it is "working." These ideas are simply not true. In fact, painful or strenuous exercise done prematurely can slow rehabilitation by causing increased muscle spasm, which further restricts mobility. One more word of caution: if you are not a doctor, please consult one before attempting to rehabilitate yourself.

Knee sprains or fractures of the lower leg that require immobilization of the knee joint are not uncommon ski injuries. If your leg is immobilized in a rigid cast or other dressing and/or you are instructed not to bear weight on it, you can still start doing certain exercises. One of the most frequently prescribed and important exercises for knee rehabilitation is the Quadriceps Set exercise 49. It's done as an isometric holding contraction, so that you contract the thigh muscles without having to move the knee joint.

Your doctor may instruct you to do this exercise while your cast is still on. To do it is simply a matter of tightening the thigh and kneecap. It usually helps to do it first with the normal leg, and to place your hand lightly on your lower thigh and kneecap to feel the firmness in your thigh when you contract the muscles. Hold the tightened position for 5 seconds and then relax it completely before you repeat it. If you place a small rolled towel underneath your knee, it will give you something to push down against. Remember that the work has to be done by the muscles in the front of the thigh, not the muscles behind the knee. Don't be surprised if your doctor or therapist instructs you to do this "Quadriceps Setting" for several hundred repetitions in a day.

Another one of the early rehabilitation exercises is called "straight leg raising", a variation of exercise 47. Whereas the previous exercise can be done while standing, sitting, or lying down, the straight leg raising is done while lying on your back. The exercise consists of keeping your leg fully extended and lifting it toward the ceiling as high as you can while maintaining the straight knee position. It helps to think of doing the Quadriceps Set first and then raising the leg toward the ceiling. This too, may be done with a cast still on.

Since your overall level of activity will be limited, you won't get the chance to use your uninjured leg too much either. Keep up the strength in that leg by doing the "straight leg raising" exercise with or without weights on your ankle. Sit on the edge of a bed or chair and do some knee extension exercises by straightening the knee fully with or without added weights (51); and try to do some pelvic tilt and partial sit-up exercises, as shown in Chapter 14, to keep your abdominal muscles strong.

If your ankle is free to move and your doctor gives the okay, do circling motions with both feet. This is especially important for your circulation if you are off your feet for a long time. If your doctor suggests that you will be using crutches later on, you can begin to develop the arm strength that you'll need for using them by doing "chair push-ups." This is another one of the motions that is rarely used in everyday activities and tends to be poorly developed in most people. Use your arms to raise yourself off a chair seat. Stay in the air for 5 seconds. Lower slowly, then repeat.

Bed Exercises: If you are in leg traction you can still practice this arm development by pushing your elbows down hard into the mattress as your back and shoulder blades arch slightly up off the bed. Hold this position for 5 seconds at a time. Other suggested exercises while in bed are:

1. Take a few very deep breaths, being sure to inhale and exhale fully each time. Practice Breathing Exercises, Chapter 11.

2. Push your head back into the pillow for 5 seconds.

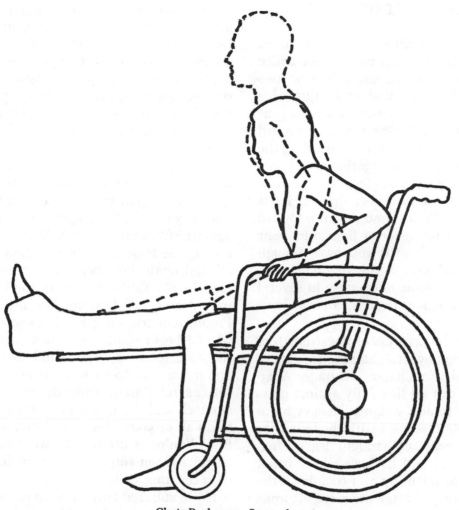

Chair Push-up to Strengthen Arms

3. Roll your head forward as if starting to sit up and hold the position for 5 seconds.

4. Hold weights (start with only 2 lbs.) and raise your arms overhead, out to the sides, and around in circles.

5. Hold weights and bend your elbows, with your arms resting on the bed and with your arms in the air.

6. Tighten the buttock muscles for 5 seconds.

7. Make circling motions with your feet.

8. Move the uninjured leg up and down, first with the knee bending and then with the knee straight. Slide your leg out to the edge of the bed and back to the center of the bed.

9. Dangle the uninjured leg over the edge of the bed to fully straighten the knee, with or without weights.

Repeat each of these exercises 5 to 10 times, twice each day. It's a good idea to ask for an over-the-bed trapeze bar to make it easier to pull yourself up in the bed and to practice "chinning" for arm strength.

WHEN YOU COME OUT OF A LEG CAST

When your cast is removed or you are out of traction and are free to start moving the entire leg, you may want to add the following two exercises. Lie on your side with your injured leg uppermost and gently bend and straighten your knee. Try it first by bringing the knee toward your chest to bend it. Later on, try bending the knee by keeping both thighs together and swinging only the lower part of the leg.

The second exercise to limber up your leg is done on your back. Try to bend the knee toward your chest. It may be easier at first to let your heel slide on the bed until you have enough strength to keep the heel in the air. In general, remember that it's better to exercise in several short sessions throughout the day rather than in one long session.

You can check the progress of the strength of your knee extension by straightening your leg to the position shown in Chapter 16 under Anatomy. When you can do this fully against gravity, you're ready to add weights. Always begin and end each weight session with the four knee exercises: quadriceps set, straight leg raising, sidelying knee bend and backlying knee bend. This allows you to warm up and cool down the leg muscles before and after the more vigorous weight lifting. Add weights a little at a time. Use the amount of weight that allows you to complete the motion ten times. If you can't complete the full extension then the weight is too heavy. Do the weight lifting exercise every other day and add weight when you can complete the ten repetitions easily. You can also use half of the normal weight to do a few warm-up repetitions before you begin.

Strengthening the knee extension muscles isn't the whole story. These same muscles must also be able to elongate sufficiently so that your knee can be actively pulled into the bent position by the hamstrings. You can stretch the knee extensors by lying on your stomach and holding a towel around your ankle to gently pull your foot toward your buttock. You can also stretch the same muscle by sitting on a chair with your ankles crossed. Apply pressure with your stronger leg to gently flex the weaker knee further. As you improve, the foot of the weaker leg will go further and further underneath your seat.

Developing the strength of the knee flexor muscles gives you the power to actively flex the knee against gravity. You can start to do this by pulling your foot back against your other foot or against an immovable rail. In this way you are raising the tension in the muscle without actually letting the knee bend. This type of isometric exercise should be done with the knee in different degrees of flexion. Try the Sitting and Prone Isometric Knee Flexion exercises, 60 and 61. To begin some active flexion that permits the knee to move, you should lie on your side and move your foot toward your buttock. Make this exercise more difficult by lying on your stomach and doing the same thing. Remember to do all of your exercises slowly and gently at first. You're ready to add weights to the last exercise when you can keep your foot in the air with the knee bent.

If you suffered only a sprain of the tendons or ligaments around the ankle, your knee strength and mobility are probably all right; but you should take the Physical Fitness Quiz in Chapter 9 to test for any tightness in the back of the leg. If your thigh and hip are weak from lack of use, do all of the recommended knee exercises and include Sidelying Upper Leg Lift, exercise 74.

To test the flexibility of the ankle and the muscles of the lower leg, compare the following movements on your injured and normal sides. Can you point your feet up, down, inward, and outward the same amount on both feet? Can you stand on the inner and outer borders of your

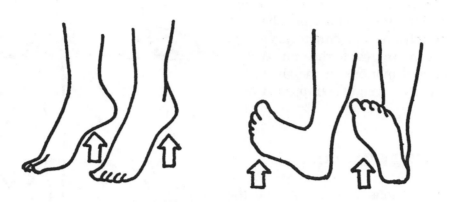

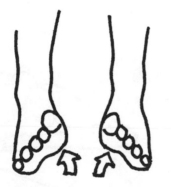 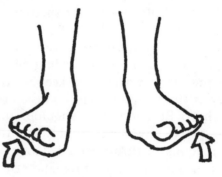

feet and on your heels? Can you do a toe stand on one leg at a time?

To improve flexibility you can start by holding a towel around your foot and pulling it toward you to stretch the muscles behind the ankle, in the calf, and possibly as far as the back of the knee. Do this towel stretching with your knee fully extended and partially bent (exercise 53). When this becomes easier, progress to the two-legged and one-legged calf stretches in Chapter 22. Practice walking upstairs backwards to encourage greater ankle flexibility.

To improve your ability to raise the forefoot toward the shin, repeat this movement over and over throughout the day. Hold the foot in the up position for a few seconds before lowering it each time. Add a small weight around the forefoot or use a weighted exercise shoe to add resistance. As explained earlier, do weight-type exercises every other day.

To improve strength in toe stands (the same muscles that give you a push-off from one foot to the other in walking), practice them first in the seated position, then standing up with two legs, then one leg at a time (exercise 90). If your problem is lack of strength in moving the foot inward or outward, start by sliding a weighted towel on the floor with the inside and outside borders of your foot. (Place a towel on a smooth floor, and place a 2–3 pound weight on one end of the towel). Be sure that you are not cheating by using motions from your hip to make the towel slide. You can progress to the same type of inward and outward motions in the air with a weighted shoe or ankle weights wrapped around the forefoot.

UPPER EXTREMITY INJURIES

Although most serious injuries involve the legs, the arms can be hurt if a skier falls on an outstretched hand or lands very hard on the shoulder itself. Very frequent injury is a sprain of the thumb, and much less frequent are sprains and fractures of the wrist or shoulder.

The shoulder can be problematical if rehabilitation exercises aren't done as soon as the doctor suggests. For the initial healing phase the shoulder may be supported by keeping the arm in a sling with the elbow bent and the arm against the chest. Restriction of shoulder motion can cause you to have some trouble in walking because it tends to throw your balance off slightly. This means that your hips and trunk are taking a little extra strain. Your neck, too, may bother you because you don't move it normally. To promote general relaxation, normal muscular work, and reduce the aching and discomfort of neckaches and backaches, follow the basic limbering regime introduced in Chapter 11.

To start exercising the shoulder, "pendulum" exercises are often prescribed. To do these exercises you must be leaning over as far as possible so that your arm can dangle freely. Hold a small weight in your hand such as a small iron and gently swing your arm forward, backward, side to side, and in circles. Let the momentum generated when you start swinging the weight carry the arm through the motions until the arm

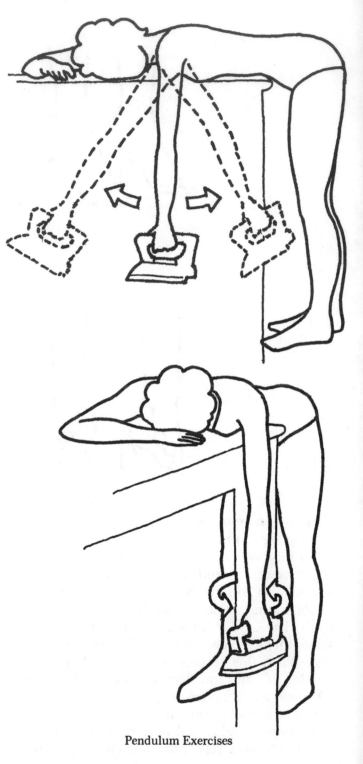

Pendulum Exercises

comes to rest by itself. Do not try to move your arm by lifting it. To be effective, this pendulum motion must be as effortless as possible.

Once some of the initial stiffness is gone, you can start strengthening exercises by powdering a smooth table top and sliding your arm all around the surface. You can also install a pulley system with a rope to use the strength from the stronger arm to pull down and raise the weaker one. This type of exercise is only beneficial once you have gained some initial flexibility in the joint from exercises like the "pendulum" exer-cises. If you use the pulley to try to force your weaker arm up in the air before it is comfort-able to do so, you may very easily create more irritation in your shoulder. As a reminder, al-ways discontinue any exercise that you feel is making you worse.

Another way to use the stronger arm for assis-tance is to lie on your back, clasp both hands together, raise them overhead, and move them from side to side and in circles. Try to touch each shoulder with the clasped hands; touch the top of your head and the back of your neck.

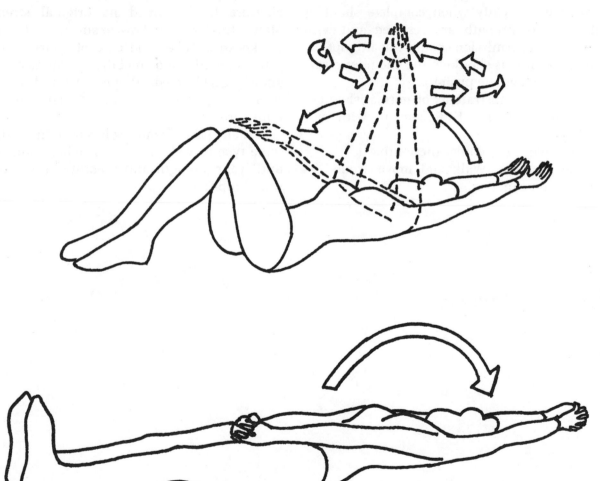

After you feel comfortable doing this lying down, try to do it sitting in a chair. Remember that you may not be able to lift as highly in the sitting position because you are now working against gravity. Further improvement will be possible when you are ready (again, always check with your doctor) to do the towel stretching exercise for shoulder rotation (exercise 7).

When you're able to raise your entire arm in the air, you're ready to raise it forward, behind you, and horizontally out to the side and across your chest with a weight held in your hand or on your wrist. Only when complete shoulder mobility and strength are restored and with your doctor's permission should you attempt the regular, strenuous shoulder and shoulder girdle exercises such as the push-ups.

Refer to the illustrations of normal shoulder movement in Chapter 13 to compare with your mobility.

In summary, remember these things:

1. Keep active. Walk and move around as much as you can.

2. Remember to move all the parts of your body that are not immobilized. Do isometric exercises whenever possible when in a cast.

3. Begin active movements of stiff joints as soon as your doctor permits it.

4. Work on the general mobility of your limbs first and develop the muscular strength later.

5. Don't return to any sport until your injured limb is as strong and flexible as the uninjured one.

Remember, your ability to perform an athletic activity again does not mean that all of the musculature has regained its original strength. Many athletes know how to substitute for these weaknesses. Take good care of yourself. Have your strength and mobility evaluated by a knowledgeable medical specialist and don't resume your sport until your strength and flexibility are normal.

6. If any part of your leg has been injured, use some type of walking aid (crutches, cane, etc.) until your strength and mobility allow you to walk limp-free.

Appendix A—About Weights

STORE-BOUGHT WEIGHTS

Weights can be purchased in a sporting goods store. Ready made weights come in a number of styles.

Shoe weights: This is a metal sole plate that straps onto your shoe. Individual metal disc weights are added to the plate by a cross bar.

Ankle weights: Lead pellets encased in a vinyl covering are fastened around the ankle with Velcro tabs. Each weight is specified in pounds. You can wear two weights on your ankle at one time to increase the poundage, but you cannot remove the contents from any weight to lighten it.

Sand Bag weights: Sand is enclosed in a canvas cover and strapped onto the ankle with Velcro closure tabs. Each weight is specified in pounds. Sand cannot be removed to lighten the weight. Only one sand bag weight can be worn comfortably at a time.

This list is not exhaustive. You may find other weights of similar design that will work well.

HOME-MADE WEIGHTS

(a) Weights can be made at home with readily available materials. Use squares of tightly-woven, durable cloth. Fill a plastic bag with sand to equal the desired number of pounds. Close the bag securely. Place the sand bag in the cloth cover that you have double-stitched on three sides. Then stitch the fourth side closed. Sew ribbons at the ends or corners of the weight to tie it onto your ankle.

(b) Take a handbag with a short strap that you can hook over your ankle. Put household objects into the bag (canned foods are convenient) until your bag holds the desired weight.

(c) Weigh your ski boots. They may be light enough to use as a starting weight, or in some cases heavy enough to progress to.

Appendix B—Instructions for Ice Massage

When to use ice massage:

Use ice massage over muscles that you are unable to stretch due to pain: *Stiff neck* that you wake up with in the morning (massage the back and sides of the neck and around the shoulder blade); *acute back spasm* (you have bent over to pick something up and feel a sudden twinge in your back muscles; your doctor has ruled out anything more serious than a muscle spasm); *any tight, overworked muscles after skiing.*

What you need:

4 ounce paper cups filled three-quarters full with water and chilled in the freezer until frozen.

To use:

Tear off about one inch of paper from the rim of the cup to expose the ice. Remove more paper to expose more ice as it melts during the massage.

Procedure:

Massage the entire muscle area with the ice. Use a circular or up-and-down stroke, but be sure to keep the ice moving at all times. If in doubt as to how much area to cover, cover more area rather than less.

Stages:

At first you will feel *cold* when the ice is first applied. After a few minutes you will feel *ache*. After about 5 minutes it will feel like a burn, and at this point remove the ice for a minute or so.

Return the ice to the skin and continue until the burning disappears (usually very quickly) and the area is numb.

The ice massage should not take longer than 7 to 10 minutes.

Now the ice massage is finished and you should immediately begin stretching exercises for the tight muscle. If someone else is applying the ice massage to you, you can start gently stretching while the massage is in progress. Stop stretching if you feel pain. If strong discomfort returns while you are stretching, repeat the icing for another couple of minutes until you can stretch again, pain-free. Repeat this procedure several times a day.

CAUTION: Do not use ice massage over areas where you have poor circulation, loss of sensation, or any abnormal condition of the skin.

Appendix C—How to Measure and Use Crutches

Crutches can be a tremendous help in getting around when you need to keep some or all of your weight off one leg. They can be a terrible nuisance and annoyance if they are adjusted incorrectly for your height or used improperly.

1. Crutches are *not* designed to jab into your armpits. Hug crutches in next to your rib cage with the inner side of your arms.

2. Your weight is taken on the hand bar, not on the underarm pad. Do not lean on the underarm pads for support.

3. For proper measurement: Stand with your shoulders in a normal, relaxed position. Place the crutch tip about 6 inches to the front and 6 inches to the outer side of your feet. At this distance the top of the shoulder pad should be 1 to 2 inches *below* your armpit. Adjust the hand bar so that your elbow is at approximately a 30-degree bend.

4. Wear sturdy shoes.

5. Use a shoulder strap bag to carry light loads.

6. Tighten crutch screws periodically.

7. Use rubber crutch tips to prevent skidding.

8. Take the crutches out from under your arms when you are going to sit down. Try to sit in chairs with arm rests to make it easier to get up.

9. Be very careful in areas where there might be water on the floor or where you find loose gravel.

10. Remove scatter rugs or other sliding area rugs to prevent slipping.

Walking Instructions:

If you are instructed to bear *no* weight on one leg:
1. Place both crutches ahead of you so that a line connecting the crutch tips and your standing leg forms a triangle.
2. Next, transfer all of your weight onto your hands and gently swing yourself past the crutches to land on your sound foot. During the swing-through keep the cast directly underneath your body or slightly ahead of it. Never swing the cast for momentum.
3. For the next step, bring both crutches forward simultaneously. Press on your hands and swing through again.
4. If you try to hop or jump through the crutches you will have more difficulty with your balance and tire very quickly.

If you are instructed to place *partial* weight on one leg:
1. Place both crutches ahead of you so that a line connecting the crutch tips and your feet forms a triangle.

2. Next, place the weaker leg forward so that your foot is in line with the crutches, some of your weight on the forefoot.

3. Transfer most of your weight onto your hands with some pressure going onto the forefoot as your strong leg steps all the way through the crutches.

4. Bring both crutches and your weaker leg forward again for the next step. In the beginning you can move the crutches into position and then the weaker foot. With practice, if your balance is good, you can place the crutches and the weaker foot forward at the same time. In most instances, the crutches are the assistance for the weaker leg, and they move when the weaker leg moves.

5. Your doctor may specify a certain amount of pressure to use with the weaker leg. Use your bathroom spring scale to see what 10, 20, or more pounds of pressure feels like.

To Sit Down:

When you reach the chair, carefully turn around and back up until your leg touches the edge of the seat. Keep one hand on the arm rest of the chair and the other hand on the crutch hand bars, as described in the following procedure.

To Stand Up:

Place both crutches together in front of one leg. Use one hand on the hand bars, the other hand on the arm rest, and push yourself up to stand. Keep your stronger foot well back and underneath you to get better leverage for standing.

Pivot the crutches inward so that you now have two crutches under one arm. When you are ready reach around with the free hand for the outermost crutch and place it under the free arm. Now you are set to walk with one crutch under each arm.

Stair Climbing:

If you are instructed to bear *no* weight on one leg:

1. Stand close to the railing with both crutches together under one arm. Grasp the rail with the other hand. Keep the weak leg in the air behind you.

2. Step up with the *stronger* leg while you bear weight on the crutch and the railing. If someone else is with you, give one crutch to him to hold.

3. At this point the weaker leg and crutch are one step below. Bring them up to the step you are now standing on.

4. Follow the same procedure step by step up the stairs.

5. If you have an unusually awkward cast, you may have to follow the same procedure facing backwards up the stairs.

If you are permitted to bear *partial* weight on one leg:

Follow the same instructions as above, but keep the weaker leg *on* the step with the crutches, not in the air.

Stair Descending:

If you are instructed to bear *no* weight on one leg:

1. Stand close to the railing with both crutches under one arm and grasp the rail with the other hand.

2. Place the crutches on the step below and lower your *weak* leg with it. Keep your foot in the air above the lower step.

3. With pressure on your hands, slowly lower yourself by stepping down with the strong leg to the step below.

4. Place the crutch tips again on the step below when you are ready for a new step down. Repeat this procedure until you reach the bottom.

5. If you have a cast, keep it in the air. Do not let it hit the edge of any step.

If you are permitted to bear *partial* weight on one leg:

Follow the same procedure as above, but when you place the crutch tip on the step below, also place your forefoot *on* the step. When you are lowering your body with the strong leg, distribute your weight between both hands and the weak leg.

Stepping On and Off Curbs:

Use the same sequence as described above for stair climbing and descending.

1. Keep one crutch under each arm as in regular walking.

2. Remember that to go up you first step up with the good leg, keeping the crutches below you on the street level, then bring the crutches up with the weaker leg afterward.

3. To go down, step off with the crutches accompanied by the weaker leg and, afterward, bring the strong leg down to the street level.

Appendix D—You and Your Plaster Cast

SKIN CARE

While the cast is on:

1. Feel and look for skin irritations at the cast edges such as redness, swelling, burning, or itching and cracking.

2. Avoid reaching up under the cast to eliminate plaster crumbs or other foreign objects. Do not scratch under the cast with any objects.

3. Do not get your cast wet. Cover it with a leakproof plastic bag when bathing. Use waterproof tape to close it tightly at the open end.

4. If you are given a sling, wear it when sitting and walking. If you are given a cast-shoe, wear it when walking.

After the cast is removed:

1. The skin may be very dry and flaky and yellow. This is caused by dead skin and oil from the skin glands.

2. Wash with mild soap and warm water. Pat dry.

3. Use mineral or olive oil and a soft cloth to gently remove the dead skin. *Do not rub.* Apply lotion to keep the skin soft and smooth.

CAST CARE

Drying:

1. Immediately after the cast is applied, expose it to the air to speed up the drying process.

2. When in bed, support the cast on pillows until it is dry.

3. Should the cast become wet after the original drying process, follow the same procedure. Have the cast checked by your physician.

WHEN TO CONSULT YOUR DOCTOR

1. If the cast becomes too snug, too loose, broken, or cracked, or if there is painful rubbing or pressure beneath it.

2. If the fingers or toes below the cast become discolored, painful, cold, numb, difficult, or impossible to move. (Some redness is normal if you have kept the limb elevated and suddenly hang it downward, as the blood rushes to the fingers or toes.)

3. If the heel of your walking cast comes off.

4. If there is a foul smell or drainage from under the cast.

EXTRA REMINDERS

1. Place a plastic bag over your cast when it rains. Carry one with you to be ready for unexpected rain showers.

2. If you decorate your cast, use water colors.

3. If your doctor tells you NO WEIGHT BEARING, he's not kidding. Keep your weight off the leg at all times.

Appendix E—Instructions for Skier's "Tennis Elbow" Exercises

GENERAL GUIDELINES

• You will need small dumbbell weights, starting with 2 or 3 pounds, or you may use a small bar-bell weight to which you can gradually add more and more weight as you need it.

• Repeat each exercise 10 to 15 times.

• When you can do 15 repetitions with ease, increase the weight by 1 pound.

• Repeat the entire program every other day (4 times a week).

Exercise 1 Wrist Extension

Starting position: Place your forearm, palm down, on a firm surface of books (or a tabletop) so that your wrist hangs freely over the edge. Grip a 2- or 3-pound dumbbell in your hand.

Action: Raise your hand upward as far as possible. Hold this position for 5 seconds. Do not lift your forearm off the books at any time. Lower your hand, wait a few seconds, and then repeat.

Muscular Work: Outside of forearm.

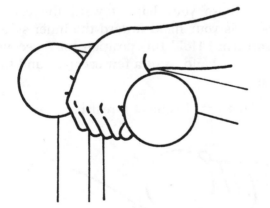

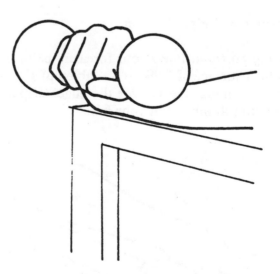

Exercise 2 Wrist Extension with Deviation

Starting position: Place your forearm, palm down, on a firm surface of books (or a tabletop) so that your wrist hangs freely over the edge. Grip a 2 or 3-pound dumbbell in your hand.

Action: Raise your hand upward and *toward the thumbside* of your hand. Hold this position for 5 seconds. Do not lift your forearm off the books at any time. Lower your hand, wait a few seconds, and then repeat.

Muscular work: Outer side of forearm and thumb side of back of wrist.

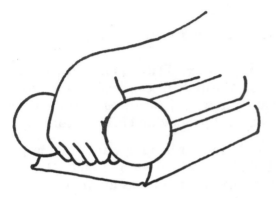

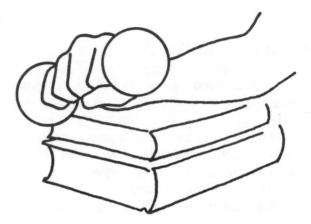

Exercise 3 Wrist Flexion

Starting position: Place your forearm, palm up, on a firm surface of books (or a tabletop) so that your wrist hangs freely over the edge. Grip a 2 or 3-pound dumbbell in your hand.

Action: Raise your hand toward the ceiling. (This curls your hand toward the inner side of the forearm.) Hold this position for 5 seconds. Lower your hand, wait a few seconds, and then repeat.

Muscular work: Inside of forearm.

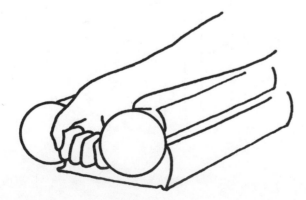

Exercise 4 Forearm Supination

Starting position: Place your forearm on a firm surface of books (or a tabletop) so that the hand gripping the dumbbell is over the edge.

Action: Begin with the palm facing downward and then rotate your forearm so that the palm then faces upward. It should take 5 seconds to complete the full rotation. Return the forearm to the starting position, wait a few seconds, and repeat.

Muscular work: Outer side of forearm and front of the upper arm.

Comments: Why are you instructed to do wrist and forearm exercises for an elbow ailment? The answer is that although the tendons of the muscles are attached to bones at the elbow joint, the muscles themselves are located in the forearm. Contracting them produces movements of the wrist and of the forearm.

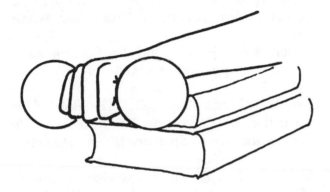

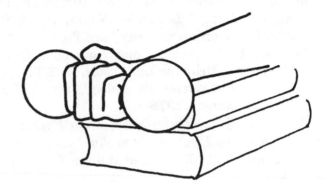

Bibliography

Abraham, H. *American Teaching Method.* The American Ski Instructors Educational Foundation Professional Ski Instructors of America

Asang, E. "Biomechanics of the Human Leg in Alpine Skiing." *Biomechanics IV,* pp. 236-242. Baltimore: University Park Press, 1974

Astrand, P.-O. "Aerobic and Anaerobic Work Capacity." *Medicine and Sport,* Vol. 9: *Advances in Exercise Physiology,* pp. 55-60. Basel: S. Karger, 1976

Basmajian, J.V. *Muscles Alive, Their Functions Revealed by Electromyography,* 2nd Ed. Baltimore: The Williams and Wilkins Company, 1974

Borg, G. et al. "Fatigue during Downhill Skiing." The Second International Conference on Ski Trauma and Skiing Safety, Sierra Nevada, April 1977

Caldwell, J. *Caldwell on Cross-Country.* Brattleboro: Stephen Greene Press, 1976

Campbell, S. *Ski with the Big Boys.* Woodbury, NY: Barron's Educational Series, Inc., 1977

Daniels, L. and Worthingham, C. *Therapeutic Exercise,* 2nd edition. Philadelphia: W.B. Saunders Company, 1977

Ellison, A.E. "Skiing Injuries" *Journal of the American Medical Association,* Vol. 223, No. 8 February 1973, pp. 917-919

Ellison, A.E. "Skiing Injuries." *Clinical Symposia,* Vol. 29, No. 1, 1977

Eriksson, A. "Force Output, EMG activity, and Selective Glycogen Depletion Pattern during Downhill Skiing." The Second International Conference on Ski Trauma and Skiing Safety, Sierra Nevada, April 1977

Exercise Testing and Training of Apparently Healthy Individuals: A Handbook for Physicians Dallas: American Heart Association, 1972

Fowler, J.A. "Fitness and Its Components." *Physiotherapy,* Vol. 63 October 1977, pp. 316-319

Garrick, J.G. and Requa, R. "The Role of Instruction in Preventing Ski Injuries." *The Physician and Sportsmedicine* December 1977, pp. 57-59

Goldspink, G. "Effect of Exercise on Muscle Fiber Size." *Medicine and Sport,* Vol. 9: *Advances in Exercise Physiology.* Basel: S. Karger, 1976, pp. 103-113

Gutman J. et al. "Ski Injuries." *Journal of the American Medical Association,* December, 1974, pp. 1423-1425

Holden, M.S. *An Instructor's Guide to Ski Mechanics.* Eastern Professional Ski Instructors of America, 1976

Hollingshead, W.H. *Functional Anatomy of the Limbs and Back,* 4th edition. Philadelphia: W.B. Saunders Company, 1976

Johnson R.J. et al. "The Inter-relationship between Ski Accidents, the Resultant Injury, the Skier's Characteristics, and the Ski Boot Binding System." *Orthopedic Clinics of North America,* January 1976, pp. 11-12

Jones, C. "The Burke Physical Training Program." *Journal of the U.S. Ski Coaches Association,* Winter 1977

Joubert, G. *Teach Yourself to Ski.* Aspen: Aspen Ski Masters, 1970

Klafs, C.E. and Arnheim D.E. *Modern Principles of Athletic Training,* 3rd edition. Saint Louis: The C.V. Mosby Company, 1973

Kraus, H. *Clinical Treatment of Back and Neck Pain.* New York: McGraw-Hill Book Company, 1970

Nagler, W. "Tennis Elbow." *American Family Physician,* Vol. 16, July 1977

Namikoshi, T. *Shiatsu Therapy.* Tokyo: Japan Publications, Inc., 1974

Nygaard, E. et al. "Glycogen Depletion Pattern in Leg Muscle during Recreational Downhill Skiing." The Second International Conference on Ski Trauma and Skiing Safety, Sierra Nevada, April 1977

Reider, B. and Marshall, J.L. "Getting in Shape to Ski." *The Physician and Sportsmedicine,* December 1977, pp. 40-45

Reynolds, T. *A Guide to Alpine Coaching.* Farmington: New Additions, 1974

Saltin, B. "Metabolic Fundamentals in Exercise." *Medicine and Science in Sports,* Vol. 5 Number 3, 1973, pp. 137-146

Sanders, R.J. "The Anatomy of Skiing and Powder Skiing." Denver: Golden Bell Press, 1976

Sorrells, R.B. "The Physician and the Novice Skier." *The Journal of the Arkansas Medical Society,* Vol. 70, December 1973, pp. 246-248

Twardokens, G. "Simulated Skiing Movements in Various Planes of Motion." International Ski Instructors Association, Banff, Canada May 1977

Westlin, N.E. "Factors Contributing to the Production of Skiing Injuries." *The Orthopedic Clinics of North America,* Vol. 7, January 1976, pp. 45-49

Williams, M. and Lissner, H. *Biomechanics of Human Motion.* Philadelphia: W.B. Saunders Company 1962

Young, L.R. et al. "The Etiology of Ski Injuries: An Eight Year Study of the Skier and his Equipment." *The Orthopedic Clinics of North America,* Vol. 7, January 1976, pp. 13-29

Zohman, L.R. and Phillips, R.E. *Medical Aspects of Exercise Testing and Training.* New York: Intercontinental Medical Book Corporation, 1973

Index